Remarkable Women of Faith

INSIGHT PUBLISHING
SEVIERVILLE, TENNESSEE

© 2007 by Insight Publishing Company.

All rights reserved. No part of this book may be reproduced in any form or by any means without prior written permission from the publisher except for brief quotations embodied in critical essay, article, or review. These articles and/or reviews must state the correct title and contributing authors of this book by name.

Disclaimer: This book is a compilation of ideas from numerous experts who have each contributed a chapter. As such, the views expressed in each chapter are of those who were interviewed and not necessarily of the interviewer or Insight Publishing.

Because the women featured in this book are from diverse backgrounds and have various viewpoints, it should be understood by the reader that the authors herein have opinions and beliefs that are dissimilar. This book is meant to share a variety perspectives regarding faith and it is not intended as an endorsement of any one particular ideology.

Published by Insight Publishing Company
P.O. Box 4189
Sevierville, Tennessee 37864

10 9 8 7 6 5 4 3 2

Printed in the United States of America

ISBN-10: 1-60013-138-7
ISBN-13: 978-1-60013-138-7

Table of Contents

A Message from the Publisher vii

Kim Wright 1

Barbara Sexton Smith 11

Amberly Neese 31

Jennifer O'Neill 39

Yvonne Conte 53

Dr. Rheba Washington-Lindsey 65

Ann Jillian 89

Reverend Diannia Baty 105

Desiree Carter 117

Charlda Sizemore 133

Maria Mullen 149

DeBee Trant 161

Kim Zweygardt 177

Jennifer Curtet 189

A Message from the Publisher

When we began working on this book project, we decided to go back to the basics—just exactly what is "faith"?

The formal definition of the word "faith," according to the Merriam-Webster online dictionary is: "Allegiance to duty or a person: loyalty; fidelity to one's promises; sincerity of intentions; belief and trust in and loyalty to God; belief in the traditional doctrines of a religion; firm belief in something for which there is no proof; complete trust; something that is believed especially with strong conviction; *especially*: a system of religious beliefs."

This is a fairly broad definition. Initially, when one thinks of faith it is strictly within the context of religion. But the dictionary gives an even broader view. When searching for remarkable women of faith, we kept this general idea of faith in mind. Within the pages of this book you will find that the remarkable women we found have faith that changed their lives. They have strong beliefs and they state them plainly.

In *Remarkable Women of Faith* you will read personal stories of women that may change your ideas about what faith means. You may be challenged by what you read. You may be fascinated with what these women have to say. And you just might learn something. I know that I did.

Get ready to be inspired. Get ready to learn. Get ready to expand your own ideas about what faith means to you. Get ready to take an honest look at what you believe in. This book could quite possibly change your life.

Interviews conducted by:
David E. Wright
President, International Speakers Network

Chapter 1

KIM WRIGHT

THE INTERVIEW

David Wright (Wright)
Today we're talking with Kim Wright. As a Bible study teacher and conference speaker, Kim Wright has a passion for God's Word and loves to see it come alive in the hearts of women everywhere. Her desire is to see women learn who they are in Christ and to understand that He is crazy about them. She does this by sharing her story, teaching His Word, and giving hope to those who want to follow Christ's will for their lives. Kim says the most remarkable thing about her is the amazing God she serves.

Even with people who grow up in the most dysfunctional families, God usually sends at least one godly Christian into their lives. Who was that for you, Kim, and how did that person influence your life, even if it was long before your own conversion?

Kim Wright
It is so difficult to put that on one person. At different times in my life it was different people in different ways. I believe God always sends those you need the most at just the right times in your life. For me there were two key people.

I was raised by my grandparents from the time I was eighteen months old until I got married at eighteen. The faithfulness of my "Granny" just "being there" had a tremendous impact on my well being. She didn't have to raise my older brother and me but chose to do so. She was there when I got off the bus. She was there when I was sick. She was there when I got hurt.

Now that I have children of my own I see what a strength and comfort she was to me because my own children see her in me. They like it when I am "just here" for them. To hear them say, "Mom, we like knowing you are home if we need you," gives me a wonderful, satisfying feeling.

She was also faithful in taking my brother and me to church every Sunday. The foundation was being laid from a very young age without my even knowing it. We would head off to our little country church where I would hear elderly pastors speak of the love Jesus has for each of us. Eventually I accepted His sacrifice at the cross and I believe it was because of a solid foundation of good biblical principles that were established early in my life.

Another person who had a tremendous impact on my life was my mother-in-law, Evelyn. For as faithful as my Granny was at seeing to it that I went to church, Evelyn was faithful in being the hands and feet of Jesus. She was Jesus with skin on for so many people. She lived out the Matthew 25 chapter of caring for people when they were sick by bringing them food and company, visiting shut-ins, or giving a refreshing word of encouragement to someone who needed it. I got to see Jesus in action in today's world by watching her do His work with a joy that was contagious.

Wright
Who has been the most influential person in your spiritual life?

Kim Wright
I'm not sure that it is as much a person who has had the most influence on my spiritual life as it has been circumstances. Looking back on my faith journey, the times when I would have tremendous spiritual growth spurts would be when I would overcome some obstacle or event. Those "valley" times happen for a reason and I believe the Lord puts them there to help us grow in our faith.

The things that I have been allowed to experience in life (e.g., dysfunctional family life, victimization, loss, troubled marriage, miscarriage) have given me tremendous opportunities to help others who are going or who have gone through similar circumstances. Although some of those things were tough to get through, they all served a purpose in that I am more caring, more understanding, and less judgmental. I can relate to people more and give them what they need to get through their circumstance. That need is the hope of Jesus Christ.

So many times it's not until you come to a place of desperation when you will see your need of Christ. Those moments when you have nothing left of yourself is when you fall face first at His feet and cry out to Him to help you.

Wright

When did you find it the hardest to keep your faith, and how did you manage to do so?

Kim Wright

It's funny because the very thing that caused my faith to waiver was ultimately the very thing that caused it to grow. I was faithfully serving in a church for several years when some things happened and I was deeply hurt emotionally. We ended up leaving and I was devastated. I had put my whole heart and soul into church and just couldn't grasp the thought of "worldly things" going on inside of what was supposed to be a safe haven. I really didn't want much to do with church after that. Not wanting anything to do with church went hand-in-hand with my relationship with Christ.

In my mind I lumped Jesus in with all of us who love the Lord and are very much saved but also very much human. I had put Jesus inside the four walls of the church building. Those of us who know Jesus very well at all know He is not an "in the box" kind of guy so He showed me Who He was outside the walls of the church. It was and continues to be a journey with all sorts of twists and turns. What an adventure! I had to learn that my faith was to be in Him and in Him alone.

I had to learn that even though people let me down, Jesus never would. The adventure continues and when eyes are fixed on the right Source, the twists and turns are manageable. I am learning more quickly to recognize when I have twisted or turned in the wrong direction and once again fix my eyes on the ultimate "Mapquester"!

Wright

What do you struggle with?

Kim Wright

Ugh, what *don't* I struggle with? Paul hit the nail on the head in his letter to the Romans, Chapter 7, when he talked about doing the things that he didn't want to do, and not doing the things he did want to do. I find myself there so many times, apologizing to the Lord for my shortcomings—feeling like I want to be a great wife and mother but failing miserably at times—snapping at one of the kids or Todd, watching something I shouldn't be watching, saying something unkind to someone, or not saying something to someone when I knew I should have, allowing fear to hold me back from stepping out in faith.

I find myself on a rollercoaster of emotions sometimes. I start to feel overwhelmed and when I feel overwhelmed I tend to "freeze" and not get any of the 101 things I need to do done. Then the stinkin' thinkin' starts—you see what I mean.

I have learned (and am still learning) that during those times I really need to step back, take a deep breath, and get to the root of the problem. The root of the problem is time. How am I managing it? How am I mismanaging it? And the real key is this: just how much personal time am I spending with God? When I am in His Word daily I find that life is not as hard to deal with. When I am communicating with Him through prayer (not just the pop-up kind either!) life is not as hard to deal with. It took me a lot of years getting frustrated with myself and other people before it really sank in—with God all things are possible! Life is hard but God is so good!

Do I struggle? Absolutely! What person doesn't? I struggle less when I lean on Him and look to Him to solve problems, calm me down, and rest in Him.

Wright

How do you know you are hearing from God?

Kim Wright

Wow, what an awesome question! I think that in my earlier years as a new Christian I didn't think I was good enough to ever hear from God. I mean, after all, He gave His Son to die for me, how could I ask Him to have a relationship with me? Not that I didn't want to. It was more like I didn't know how to nor did I think the Creator of the universe would want to talk with me. After all, who was I?

Not until I started to read His Word and begin to understand His love for me did I realize that He—the Creator of the universe—wants to talk with me, spend time with me, know what I'm thinking, and show me what He's thinking. He wants to guide me through and see me living an abundant life until it overflows onto those who desperately need Him.

So, how do I know I am hearing from God? I know it's Him by getting to know Him—His nature, His character, His attributes, and His truths. I have to saturate myself so much in His Word that when I ask a question I recognize the answer is from Him. God will never ask you to do something that is contrary to His nature (like lie). And you will know His nature by reading about Who He is in the Bible.

We also have to be sensitive to what is going on around us. He will answer through many different avenues. It cracks me up to know that I will be asking Him about something that I ran across in a Bible study I am doing and inevitably I will hear something either though Christian radio or through a sermon or through a small group that answers the question I asked. He is so cool!

There have been times when I felt like He was calling me to do something and I stepped out in faith to do it only to have it backfire! Ever been there? Did I hear Him right? I would find out later that I did do what He wanted me to do—things didn't backfire but events had to happen the exact way He wanted them to.

For example: We had left a church and had been gone for about three years. In the study I was doing at the time I really felt the Lord telling me we were to go back there. I couldn't believe it because I had been so hurt there; but as I told my husband it was so crazy that it had to be God. So back we went. We visited a couple of times only to be told that we were not welcome back there!

I went to the Lord, confused and wondering if I had heard Him wrong. He showed me that by going back and having the door shut by them (and ultimately Him) opened the doors for other ministries to take place that never would have had we been there. We would have always wondered if we were really supposed to be there and now we knew beyond a shadow of a doubt we were not. What seemed like my needing to have my hearing tuned was really God answering questions that I had had in my heart for years!

Wright

So many women fill their lives with trying to be a good church member and volunteer, a good wife, a good mother, a good employee and they often think that they are limited to these areas. What was the turning point when you realized that God's will for your life involved reaching out beyond your church and your family to speak to women across the community and across the country?

Kim Wright

Have you ever had one of those "Ah ha!" moments, when out of seemingly nowhere you just "get it"? You've heard it over and over again—"God loves you," "You are radiantly beautiful to Him." You are supposedly living it. Oh, you say you're His child but down deep you just can't grasp it. But all of a sudden you start to *believe* what the great *I Am* is telling you. That "Ah ha!" moment is one that I will never forget.

I was driving home from a counseling session one day and we had been discussing my childhood. Because I lived with my grandparents from a very young age, I didn't see my dad very often. When I did see him he would tell me I was getting a little pudgy or would talk about my complexion (something all teenage girls "love" to have pointed out). I never felt simply loved by him. I felt that it wouldn't have mattered what I did or how great I looked, it still would not have been good enough to meet his criteria.

God showed me during my "Ah ha!" moment that I was equating my earthly father with Him. The Holy Spirit just spoke to my heart and over the course of the next few weeks and months I started to believe what God told me in His Word—to believe that I am the very apple of His eye, that He loves me with an everlasting love (yes, even with a few extra pounds and some zits!).

Right then I wanted every woman to feel what I was feeling—to know that God loves them that much too! When I had that revelation, I knew what I had to do. God placed a dream in my heart to go and speak to as many women as I possibly could and share with them that He is crazy in love with them even with their shortcomings. And He loves us so much that He doesn't want to leave us there—He wants us to grow in Him and desire Him and understand who we are in Him! I love to speak at conferences and see other women experience "Ah ha!" moments for themselves. I stand back and humbly say, "Only You, God—only You!"

Wright

When you lose focus or become afraid, how do you regain your confidence to continue your mission?

Kim Wright

When I lose focus or become afraid, I find that a couple of different things can be going on: I am too busy "doing" and not "being." By that I mean I get caught up in all the activity of ministry and family and house, etc. that I lose track of the amount of time I have spent just simply "being" in His presence. Time with Him is so important, no matter what ministry you have or how big your family is or what world crisis you have to solve between your teenage daughters. God loves it when we are doing His kingdom's business but He loves it even more when we just kick back and spend some quiet time with Him for no other reason than, "Just because I love You, Lord."

I learned early on about the tremendous warfare that goes on when one has made a decision to stand firm and do what God has called one to do. So when the enemy does not like what I am doing, he will try to keep me distracted or put a spirit of fear in my heart. When I know that I have been spending good quality time with God and I still feel distracted or afraid I know that I am making the enemy angry—praise God! I am doing exactly what the enemy doesn't want me to do. When that happens I pray that God will give me the strength to see whatever I am doing at the time through to its completion. I praise Him that He is bigger than the enemy. I ask Him to take the spirit of fear away and if it doesn't go away I ask that He guide me through.

I really feel that God gives us the ability to push past fear when we are doing what He has called us to do. If you had asked me a few years ago if I would be speaking to women's groups all over the country and traveling by myself, I would have laughed and said, "No way!" But when God ordains it, He gives the strength to see it through.

Wright

Once you acknowledged that you had a message to share, what was the most significant change you experienced in your daily life and routine?

Kim Wright

I was always a "behind the scenes" type of person, not wanting to draw too much attention to myself. (My husband always wanted me to teach Sunday school with him and I never would because I didn't want to stand up in front of everyone having them looking at me!) Now, for most of the conferences I do I am the main speaker! Go figure—the Lord calls us to do the things we aren't comfortable doing! So that has been a big adjustment for me.

I would have to say that my daily life for the most part has stayed the same with the exception of when I am preparing to speak or write. When I have a deadline to meet I have to rearrange things a bit as far as finding the time to prepare and write. I still have to wipe noses (and booties), pick up kids from school and practices, make cookies, etc. My kids really don't see me as anything but their mom which is wonderful. Of course they don't like it much when I have to kick them off the computer so I can work on something! ☺

Wright

As a wife, mother of five children, Sunday school teacher, and Bible study leader, what do you pray for most often?

Kim Wright

This may sound like I am full of myself at first, but I really pray most often that God will help me to be all that He created me to be. In praying that prayer I have discovered that everything else falls into place. When God extends His grace and helps me be all that I am created to be, then I can be the best wife to Todd that I need to be, which in turn encourages him. I can be the best mom that I was created to be so my kids see their mom as a good role model, which encourages them to in turn be all they can be. I can be the best Sunday school teacher and Bible study leader, which in turn gives me the strength, energy, and passion to help other women be all they can be. It really does start with each of us individually.

Now, in saying that, I do pray for other things. I pray that my marriage stays strong and that my love for my husband stays strong. I pray that my kids have hearts that intimately know the Lord. I pray for the ladies in the different classes I teach—that they will dive into His Word and learn who they are in Him.

Wright

How has your prayer life changed as you have grown and matured in your relationship with Christ?

Kim Wright

I can remember very early on in my Christian walk reading the verses that say to ask for anything you want and it will be given to you. My young Christian thoughts were, "Wow, no one told me I would have my own 'Genie in a bottle'! Mamma wants a new car and poof! There it is!" I very quickly came to realize that is not what those verses mean. Somehow I skipped the part about abiding in Him and His Word abiding in me! Oh, and the part about keeping His commands—who knew that was there! When we abide in Him (the Vine as John Chapter 15 talks about) we will ask for and desire the things that are Christlike. So I think my prayer life has changed in that the closer I get to the Lord the more I desire what He desires even though in my own selfish nature it may not be what I would have prayed for initially.

Don't get me wrong, I know that I am not where I need to be, but praise the Lord, I am not where I was. I am growing in Him each day and desiring Him more and more each day.

Wright

Where do you see God leading you long-term?

Kim Wright

Wow! Who can really know? I really feel like the Lord will busy my schedule as the kids get older and more self-sufficient. He and I have been talking about a Bible study I am to write. Honestly, I don't look too far ahead. I have found that taking it day by day, one conference at a time, one chapter at a time is best for me. I know that I am doing what He has called me to do today and I trust Him enough to tell me the next step. I have learned that He stretches me enough to keep me leaning on Him but not enough to scare me away! Only the Master really knows what the future holds. I just pray that whatever He asks of me, I'll obey and wherever He leads, I'll go.

God bless you!

About the Author

KIM WRIGHT has the life experience of twenty-three years of marriage. She and Todd have five children ranging in age from twenty-two to three (yes, God has a sense of humor!). She serves in her home church as Sunday school teacher, Bible study teacher, and lay counselor. Kim's teaching style is refreshingly honest, open, compassionate, and straight from the Word of God. She can make you laugh and make you cry—sometimes all at once! She peppers her teaching with humor, energy, humility, and grace. Kim founded The Water's Edge Ministry to encourage others to jump in and experience the abundant life God has for them.

Kim Wright
Bible Teacher/Conference Speaker
The Water's Edge Ministry
P.O. Box 91
Maineville, Ohio
Phone: 513.899.4962
E-mail: kim@thewatersedgeministry.com
www.thewatersedgeministry.com

Chapter 2

BARBARA SEXTON SMITH

THE INTERVIEW

David Wright (Wright)
Barbara Sexton Smith gives more than 250 presentations in any given year and has helped raise more than $189 million during the past twenty years for the Fund for the Arts, Metro United Way, Louisville Olmsted Parks Conservancy, the National Conference for Christians and Jews, and the West Louisville Boys and Girls Choirs. She also founded *Quick Think Inc.* whose vision is "To teach you how to get others to do what you want!"

Her clients include General Electric, Norton Healthcare Nissan, Brown-Forman, Steel Technologies, Kentucky Fried Chicken, and Alcoa. In 1996 she was nominated for the Ernst & Young Entrepreneur of the Year Award. Along the way she has helped raise seven children and managed to make sure that 450,000 school children have an arts experience every year.

Barbara was appointed by Mayor Jerry Abramson to serve on the Metro Louisville Air Pollution Control District Board of Directors. Her other volunteer roles include: Voter Outreach Program, Downtown Police Advisory Board, Alcoa Community Advisory Board, Simmons College of Kentucky Board of Trustees, Interfaith Community Hunger Project, and King Memorial Walk—Service for Peace.

As a member of the International Speakers Network and the National Speakers Association, Barbara is a highly sought-after speaker who inspires every audience, every time!

Barbara welcome to *Remarkable Women of Faith.*

Barbara Sexton Smith (Sexton Smith)
Thanks David, I'm looking forward to our conversation.

Wright
Barbara, I understand that your mother was born in Fightin' Holler and grew up in Louisville at the Kentucky Baptist Orphanage. Is it true that she met your dad on a blind date?

Sexton Smith
That's a great question. I can't believe we started with that. Yes, Mother was born in Fightin' Holler which is located in Gatliff, Kentucky, right in the coal mining camps down near Eastern Kentucky. Her daddy died when she was five years old and she and her brother and sisters were sent to two different orphanages.

One of my favorite childhood stories was when Mom would tell me about how she met Dad. At the Kentucky Baptist Orphanage for sixteen-year-olds, as you can imagine, dating was frowned on. Mom had to be extremely careful when she agreed to meet my dad on a blind date. Flossie, another orphan, who was dating Uncle Stuart, my dad's older brother, set the whole thing up. Mom would tell me how handsome Dad looked as he stepped out of the car in his VPI school uniform. He was studying to be an engineer at Virginia Polytechnic Institute and I can't imagine VPI's finest coming all the way to Kentucky to meet some orphan on a blind date!

Wright
Was it love at first sight?

Sexton Smith
I think she loved the uniform! Love came the following spring in her senior year of high school when Mom was forced to make one of those real tough choices that tend to change your life forever.

Wright

Did she rely on her good old Baptist upbringing to make that choice?

Sexton Smith

Let me tell you what happened and you decide. By way of formal written invitation Dad requested Mom to be his date for the VPI Annual Spring Formal. (Dating had moved into dancing!) As you can imagine, the housemother had a very bad reaction to the very thought of one of her orphans going to a dance!

Wright

Did your mother ever get to read the letter of invitation?

Sexton Smith

Oh yes, and was she ever in trouble! When my grandmother discovered Mother wasn't going to be permitted to go to the Spring Formal she requested an appointment with the housemother at the orphanage. She wanted to defend her son's impeccable reputation and demand an explanation.

Wright

Your grandmother probably got a good dose of Sunday school when she arrived.

Sexton Smith

Not quite. As my grandmother would tell it, the car pulled up and the orphanage windows were full of little children and teenage girls peering through the glass to see what would happen. Everyone in the place knew what was going on.

Helen Perkins Sexton arrived in her normal fashion. Full-length fur coat, silk stockings, high heels, painted lips, red nails, and carrying what we grandkids always referred to as the "Infamous Gold Cigarette Holder!" That's right! Nonnie proceeded to sit there actually waiting for someone to light that cigarette! Heaven forbid—she's single (my grandfather had recently passed away).

Wright

Is this where your mom had to make the first life-changing choice you mentioned?

Sexton Smith

Yes, my grandmother gave it her best shot but the housemother informed my mom that if she accepted that invitation she could not come back to the orphanage. Whoops, ding-a-ling! No place to live!

Mother was a senior in high school preparing to go to college in the fall. This had been her only home since she was seven years old. A Jewish family came to Mom's rescue. The story was shared with someone who found a family who offered my mother a place in their home until she moved into the Kentucky Baptist School of Nursing dormitory to begin her college career.

There's an interfaith connection to get us started on this *Remarkable Women of Faith* journey we're taking today!

Wright

Wow! What a shock that must have been for your mom. How did this interfaith connection play out in your childhood?

Sexton Smith

As far as the shock goes, Mom never really talked about it in those terms. She never said negative things about the housemother's decision or about her Baptist upbringing. But she always emphasized how kind and accepting the Jewish family was. That story has resonated with me my entire life. Although I was raised in a Christian home, I remembered that story and it made me realize that we must always strive to reach across our differences regardless of what they are.

As far as my childhood, I can only remember one time when Bobby, Sara, Mom, Dad, and I went to church together. Unfortunately, as we were leaving, Dad discovered that someone had mistakenly taken his coat. He didn't want to embarrass the gentleman so Dad agreed to return the following week and serve as an usher so he could switch the coats during the service without anyone knowing! That was the last time we went to church as a family.

Wright

Tell us a little bit about your faith walk during your teen years.

Sexton Smith

Although Mom was a charter member of the newly built United Church of Christ near our home, we did not regularly attend. It seemed that every time I was dropped off at Sunday school I was being introduced as "the new kid." We didn't go enough and this created tremendous anxiety for me, as you can imagine. All I ever wanted was to just fit in. I just wanted to belong somewhere. As far as my teen years go, Mom made sure that each of us went through the obligatory confirmation classes. In the United Church of Christ when you're thirteen you go through Confirmation Class for one year. I am proud to announce I memorized the twenty-third Psalm and that was that.

Wright
What do you mean, "That was that"?

Sexton Smith
That was about all I got out of that experience. I became indifferent. When you're indifferent you're numb. You don't feel anything. You have no emotions. Indifference breeds spiritual bankruptcy.

I decided as a teenager that scientific explanations made much more sense. You see, I wasn't fitting in anywhere. The church thing wasn't ringing true for me. At least I could get my arms around the science and understand it.

My parents never jumped in to try to persuade me one way or the other until one night, and I'll never for get this. Preparing to talk with you today brought back a lot of memories for me. I'll never forget the night I asked my dad, who was Chief Engineer at American Air Filter, to back me up on this whole science thing. I thought, "Dad's an engineer! Surely he'll go for this! After all, he never went back to church after the missing coat caper."

I asked Dad what he believed. "Do you go by science or are you going with the stuff we were taught in church?"

"Well," he said, "you have to believe, it's just that simple." He said, "Barbs, I don't have all the answers, nobody does. But something—someone—much greater than all of us had to make all of this possible. Just believe."

Wright
Those are some pretty powerful words. What did you say?

Sexton Smith
I was only eighteen years old. I didn't know what to do with that. My dad had never made eye contact with me for that long but I knew in that moment he had said something that would stick with me.

This reminded me of a time when we were little kids. Dad gave each of us a marble that had a little gold band around it that read, "Do unto others as you would have others do unto you." I still have my marble.

Wright
While some folks cannot remember a time when they didn't believe, others tell stories of the moment they first believed. Tell us about yours.

Sexton Smith
Believe me, you don't know God is all you need until God is all you've got! I cut my first deal with God as I was staring down the business end—the barrel—of a sawed-off shotgun begging for my life!

In 1980 I was working at Wendy's here in Louisville as an assistant manager. Three months into the job and we got robbed on a Saturday night! You read these stories in the paper all the time. Four teenagers were cleaning up while I was in the office completing the nightly paperwork.

All of a sudden the place went wild—loud noises, screaming, and someone pounding on the office door yelling as loud as he could, "Open the door or I'll blow her brains out!"

I had no choice. I opened the door and there he stood. He threw those kids on the floor and he told me to open the safe and give him all the money. I turned around and tried to open the safe but by that time he had already hit me several times. Blood was flying everywhere and I couldn't see the numbers on the safe. I kept twirling the dial, he kept hitting me, and the more I tried to hit those numbers, the harder he would hit.

Then all of a sudden he grabbed my ponytail, shoved my face into the barrel of that sawed-off shot gun, called me all kind of colorful names, and said, "Look—! You've got one more chance. You're going to open that safe now or I'm going to blow your brains out and all these kids are going to follow."

I thought, "Oh____! What am I going to do?" I knew I hadn't hit any of the numbers on the dial. Eric was laying face down saying "Our Fathers" and "Hail Mary's" as fast as he could go and there I stood clueless. No faith.

Wright

It sounds like things were happening pretty fast. What did you do next?

Sexton Smith

Keep in mind, I didn't believe in anything at this point. And then I remembered my dad's advice. I turned around, put my hand on that safe, and cut my first deal with God. I'm kind of embarrassed to say it that way but I was young. I prayed silently, saying, "You know, people say you're out there. People say you're great and powerful, omniscient, and can do anything. If you're out there, please come in here right now and open this safe. It's not about me. It's about these teenagers! If you don't open this safe this guy is going to kill these kids and that's not right. It's not about me! If you're out there, help me help them!"

David, that safe opened! I didn't do it—God did it! I handed the thief the money bag and prayed for our lives as he stood in the doorway pointing that gun at each of us. He left. As I stood there looking at those kids with blood and tears streaming everywhere, I knew our lives had been changed forever. All I could think about was how happy I was he didn't get the kids' payroll checks that were in my pocket! They needed that money. They worked hard!

Wright

What a story! I guess this made a true believer out of you?

Sexton Smith

Well no, I wish that it had. As we often do, I decided not to act on my feelings. At the time I was filled with the Spirit but soon those feelings began to dissipate and I got a little cocky. I started thinking, "Okay, I'm in charge. I can do this on my own." A situation like that is when God steps in. Just when you think you can do it on your own, God steps in and moves your cheese!

Wright

"Moves your cheese," what do you mean?

Sexton Smith

Who Moved My Cheese was written by Dr. Spencer Johnson and published in 1998. It's an allegory that gives four typical reactions to change in one's work and life. Just when you think everything in life is just the way you want it, God changes things! He changes your situation. Sometimes it feels good and sometimes it doesn't. But it always contains one or more of life's little lessons. In the fullness of time it all works to your advantage if you just believe. You can't fight it. Change is how He gets your attention.

Wright

You sound as though your cheese has been moved a lot. Has it?

Sexton Smith

Are you kidding? I've been totally bankrupt twice—once with a two-year old child to take care of. I know what it's like to be on food stamps and government issued food for six months at a time. I learned how to be one of those people calling to say, "Hello there, I'm calling for the American Council for the Blind. We're going to have a truck in your neighborhood on Tuesday. Do you have some magazines, clothes, or household items we could pick up?" You know the pitch. It was the only job I could get working out of my home. No transportation. Couldn't afford childcare. The system had me beat! I lost my job as the National Franchise Director for the Fresher Cooker. I lost my salary, company car, health benefits, and retirement plan. My husband moved out of town for what he described as a great career opportunity working for Lee's Famous Recipe Fried Chicken! Was my cheese moved? I'd say so!

I turned fifty this year. It seems that the older I get, the more the cheese gets moved! I've gotten to the point where I just look for it—I embrace change because I know therein lies an opportunity to test my faith. Maybe I'll learn something I need to know. We've got to be open and ready to receive His Word and His gifts at all times, even when it doesn't feel good.

Wright

What role has adversity played in your life?

Sexton Smith

Adversity is probably the greatest teacher of all. Most of my best and hardest lessons in life have come on the heels of an adverse situation. One of my very favorite Bible verses is in Deuteronomy—*"The eagle stirs up the nest so that the young might learn to fly"* (Deuteronomy 32:11). I really do believe that. I believe we're transformed by trouble—the harder the test, the greater the testimony!

Many times adversity is simply a precursor to something really big yet to come.

Wright

Will you share a time in your life when you experienced an adverse situation that turned into something really big?

Sexton Smith

Sure. Back in 2000, the West Louisville Boys Choir learned that their European concert tour had been cancelled due to lack of funding. These were thirty-one African-American kids ages eight to eighteen living in some very impoverished situations. They tried to raise the money on their own but they came up short. After seeing the story on television I felt a very strong "calling" to do something to help them.

Wright

What do you mean by a very strong "calling?"

Sexton Smith

I used to hear people talk about being "called" to do something in church. I never understood why I never got "called." Oh, I got called plenty of times—I just never answered. This time was different. God was telling me to find McDaniel Bluitt, founder and director of the choir. This is when I learned that you don't play *Jeopardy* with Jesus! That's right! When God makes a statement, don't respond with a question. Just do it! Nike had this right from the very beginning!

McDaniel told me the organization was about more than music. He kept saying it is sounds of hope. He said, "We try to instill hope in the hearts of these young men." He quoted the Bible verse, "As a man thinketh in his heart so is he" (Proverbs 23:7). He told me that the choir began as a crime prevention program giving kids something positive to do after school—something to keep them out of the streets and out of harm's way.

We began a new fundraising campaign but doors kept being slammed in our faces. I told McDaniel, "Look, it's between you, me, and God! If you think together we can do this, let's go for it."

He said, "Count me in!" My husband told us to ask Bob Hill, a writer with *The Courier-Journal* newspaper, to write our story—"Sounds of Hope!"

Oh Baby! Things started hopping! In response to Bob's article, more than 400 people mailed envelopes with money to help save the trip! The West Louisville Boys Choir toured London, England, and Paris, France!

When the choir returned to America, the President of the University of Louisville hosted a reception so that the Board of Trustees and the 400 donors could meet the boys, listen to stories, and hear them sing. As a result, the University of Louisville promised full college scholarships to every choir member who stayed in the choir through high school and stayed out of trouble with the law. In my opinion that's a big thing. In May 2007, O'Farrell Head became the first to graduate on this program from the University of Louisville.

Wright

Do you find it hard to share your faith journey with others?

Sexton Smith

No, absolutely not.

Wright

How do you break it down for those who seem to have trouble finding their way?

Sexton Smith

I talk about the *Power of Five*.

Wright

The *Power of Five*—what is that?

Sexton Smith

For starters, five is a very powerful number. It shows up everywhere! The *Power of Five* is built around five areas of understanding.

1. Knowledge
2. Passion
3. Communication
4. Interest
5. Action

First you must have *Knowledge* of the universal mission and understand how your personal vision relates to it.

The *Passion* piece comes into play when you can sincerely believe and support your personal vision with every fiber of your being.

Then you must become a raconteur and *Communicate* your vision in a way that conveys the dream you're trying to share.

Number four is probably the most important part: *Interest.* You've got to remember it's not about you—it's about others. What are they interested in? You've got to connect your dream to the emotional center of the person with whom you are speaking. You've got to know where they're comin' from.

Fifth, you've got to take *Action.* You've got to actively build relationships with people. That's the only way you can do it. We are all connected! God's strategy is a connected strategy. My dream is for everyone to walk in rhythm—for everyone to join the journey and take a spiritual walk with God.

Wright

You seem to focus a lot on others. How important is this?

Sexton Smith

I think it's everything. I call it "servanthood." Everyone should strive to become a servant-leader in their business as well as in their personal lives.

Wright

What is a servant-leader?

Sexton Smith

A servant-leader is someone who leads with his or her head, heart, and hand.

Wright

How do you do that?

Sexton Smith

Head. Heart. Hand. First, think about what is important. What do you want to be remembered for? What legacy do you want to leave? Then go to your heart and feel the passion. Now you're ready to take action! Thoughts without passion are simply figments of your imagination. Passion without action is simply a dream; but action changes lives!

Wright

What drives you?

Sexton Smith

I'm driven by the Wake-Up Call! When I get that Wake-Up Call, it's the same one you got this morning. I don't question a thing. I get up, put my feet on the floor, and I say, "Send me in Coach, I'm ready to go." We all play the most important sport there is—it's the game of life! There's only one Coach and his name is God!

Wright

I've seen you in action and your energy is contagious. I heard you speak one day and bring the entire audience to their feet as you filled the room with excitement and enthusiasm. Where does it all come from?

Sexton Smith

That's a great question. I drink a lot of coffee. (Just kidding!) I get asked that question all the time. The other day I told someone they were selling it at church and I bought some! We just laughed! But you know what—I think that is where it comes from. If you don't get jazzed at church, it's time to look for another church! I love church and church loves me!

Wright

Where do you worship?

Sexton Smith

I've been visiting St. Stephen Baptist Church, the largest African-American church in our region, for three years to hear Dr. Kevin W. Cosby teach the Word. I was baptized in 1986 at Highland Baptist Church at a time in my life when I was lost. As I grew in my faith, my confidence rose to the point where I felt comfortable enough to venture out into the world. I wanted to see if I could carry the message. Could I be an instrument of peace? Could I help bridge the divide in my community?

Wright

Do you think it is necessary to go to a place of worship?

Sexton Smith

Absolutely! It's analogous to going to the gym. Want results? Ya gotta go! I never lost one pound just talking about going to the gym. Ya gotta work it baby!

Wright

What about sharing testimonies? Do we have to do that too?

Sexton Smith

Of course, that's the whole reason anything happens! No matter what happens, there's a story in there that needs to be shared. God set it up this way so we could learn from each other. We experience each other in everything.

Wright

So, do you believe God sets everything up?

Sexton Smith

Yes. He places us all here in different bodies connected by one soul. God's strategic plan is based on a connected strategy. You cannot fully know yourself until you differentiate and experience all there is. Nothing matters in and of itself. Without the Father I am nothing. We are all One.

Wright

Some people think you wake up when you're born and you go to sleep when you die. What do you believe?

Sexton Smith

I believe in the *dash!* You know, that little mark on your tombstone between your birth date and date of death! I believe we get a lot of them. Life begets life and cannot know death. I call this the Life-Death Cycle. We keep coming back until we learn all the lessons. Until we reach total awareness. Each *dash* is an opportunity to re-create your grandest vision of yourself and to become that vision. What are you doing with your *dash?*

Wright

How do you maintain this peak emotional state you seem to have?

Sexton Smith

I use the Rhythm Method. Now don't be misled. I'm talking about a system that I developed for myself that anyone can follow. I call it *The Rhythm Method of Worth Control.* I believe you determine your self-worth by the rhythm you choose every day, it's that simple. We cannot choose what happens throughout the day, but we have complete power over choosing how we will feel about it and what we will do about it. I call it the big "A." It's all in your attitude! You have to get up and feel the rhythm of the day and then create your own. You begin by thanking God for giving you another day. After all, He is the CEO. There's only one company and her name is Earth. We've got one CEO and He gets to make all the big decisions such as who lives and who doesn't. The rest is up to us!

Wright

So is it His rhythm or your rhythm that you work with?

Sexton Smith

Now that's a thought-provoking question. You've got to have a Rhythm Others Can't Knock. I call it my R-O-C-K. You've got to have a solid foundation. If you build your house on a R-O-C-K it will stand forever. All other ground is sinking sand. Then of course you've got to watch out for rhythm makers and rhythm breakers throughout the day. You're going to spend all day running into both of them.

Wright

Do you think attitude is the key to getting this rhythm thing going?

Sexton Smith

No, although I talk a lot about attitude I don't think it is the whole key. I think this rhythm thing all stems from H-O-P-E—Having Only Positive Expectations. HOPE breeds an attitude of possibility, which in turn breeds self-confidence and self-confidence is the power within that gives you the will to achieve a greater purpose.

Wright

What do you think the greater purpose is?

Sexton Smith

The greater purpose is part of God's master plan. My husband asked me about this the other day because he and I have different views. We are at different places on our spiritual journey. He asked, "So what's with this master plan you talk about all the time?"

"Well," I answered, "I think God went on a retreat. I think He wrote a strategic plan just like the rest of us do from time to time. The only difference is His plan runs the test of time. The ones we write tend to fall apart. I'm going with His plan!"

Wright

Do you believe in a universal mission?

Sexton Smith

Absolutely! I believe the universal mission is for all of us to leave the earth a little better than how we found it. Keep in mind, *"Where there is no vision the people perish."*

Wright

This is a good time to ask this question. What is your personal mission statement?

Smith

My personal mission is to instill hope in the hearts of everyone I meet. I think you can enrich the lives of others by instilling hope in their hearts. At the risk of repeating myself, remember it's not about me. It's about them. It's about others.

Wright

If you could change one thing what would it be?

Sexton Smith

One thing in the entire world? I would eliminate all racism and classism distinctions that divide our country.

"Four score and seven years ago our fathers brought forth onto this continent a new nation, conceived in liberty, and dedicated to the proposition that all men are created equal."

We live under one God in a divided nation. I want to change that. I know these are controversial things to say. I get out here every day and see people who are satisfied with the way things are and I see people who are not. I see people who benefit from education and those who do not. I see people who are hungry and people who are not. On any given day I see those who believe we are separated by class and then there are people who don't think we are. Then there are people all over this nation—right here in my own community—who believe race is not an issue. Then there are people who do think that race is an issue. I think the *Power of Five* comes back into play here. You've got the five "Rs" this time.

Wright
What are the five "Rs"?

Sexton Smith
The five Rs are:

Recognize the
Reality and
Receive the
Responsibility to
Reshape our nation.

Wright
Do you think we have made progress since August 28, 1963, when Dr. Martin Luther King Jr. gave his *I Have a Dream* speech?

Sexton Smith
That's a loaded question. Although we've made progress, the march needs to continue all day every day by everyone if we want the dream to live. I'm so very connected to Dr. King in many ways, beginning with the fact that we share the same birthday. I was born on January 15, 1957. I too have a dream. I dream there will come a day when everyone will get outside themselves and focus on enriching the lives of other people every day.

I've even thought about starting a new kind of Birthday Club. When it's your birthday, don't sit around wondering if you're going to get a card, a cake, or whatever! Get outside yourself and do something for someone else on that day.

This past January 15, our local *Service for Peace* organization coordinated 2000 volunteers conducting numerous service projects throughout our community in honor of Dr. Martin Luther King Jr.'s birthday.

Why wait? Do something like this on *your* next birthday in your community! Send me an e-mail. Tell me your story!

Wright

What about forgiveness? This seems to be the toughest thing of all to understand.

Sexton Smith

You've got that right. I've struggled with forgiveness and I'm sure you have too. Julian Carroll, former Governor of Kentucky, is a close friend of mine and Lacey's (he married us in his home on February 20, 1994.) Forgiveness is one lesson Julian always talked about. He said you've got to be able to truly grasp and embrace the concept of forgiveness. He said you not only have to forgive, you've got to forget, and you've got to move on. You can't hang onto it. God forgives all of our sins. The least we can do is forgive others along the way.

Wright

Any advice on jump-starting a spiritual journey?

Sexton Smith

Oh sure—keep it simple. People want to make this thing so complicated. How many times do you hear people say, "I don't have time to go to church. It's my only day off." Come on! Give me a break!

If you want to jump-start your spiritual journey believe in yourself *now!* Start right there. You've got to believe in yourself because God believes in you. He wouldn't have put you here if He didn't. Picture yourself as the person you want to be and you will become that person. Your perspective creates your thoughts and your thoughts create everything.

You need to develop a sense of belonging. Don't go this alone. Remember, I talked about how He's going to decide who lives and dies and then we get to make all other decisions throughout the day. Find something to belong to, to feel good about. We all see ourselves in relation to other people. I think identity comes from a sense of belonging. It's very important to think through where you might want to belong and where you're going to spend your time because that will ultimately become your identity.

How many times as teenagers did we hear our parents say, "Be careful what company you keep"? Well, you become your company.

Wright

Do you share your faith at work?

Sexton Smith

Absolutely! Once I gave myself permission to start doing that my life changed in so many ways. Doors everywhere started opening. I share my faith at work because it is who I am. How can I leave my faith at home when I go to the office? How can anybody do that? If you're going to be faithful in your walk, you don't leave God at home on the shelf. I tried that and He just got up and followed me anyway!

Wright

Well Barbara, do you have any closing thoughts for us today?

Sexton Smith

What I would like to leave you with is a pretty simple but powerful message that Rev. Dr. Kevin Cosby, pastor of St. Stephen Baptist Church in Louisville, gave one Sunday. Dr. Cosby shared with us what he considered to be one of the most profound conversations he had ever had with another minister and it was a conversation he had with Dr. Charles Mims Jr. Dr. Mims told Kevin there are three things that you've got to remember about doing life:

1. You have to make a life worth living.
2. You must be a self worth living with.
3. You must have something significant to do every morning when you get up.

So, I say it's up to you to create a life that matters. Make it meaningful. Find out who you are. Remember the *dash*. When your day comes and you stand in judgment, you've got to be prepared to answer what I believe He's going to ask each of us: "What did you do with the gifts I gave you this time around?" That's something to think about.

Wright

Great advice. Barbara, I really appreciate your spending all this time with me today to answer these questions. It's always delightful to talk with you, to be with you, and to watch you perform on stage. I really appreciate all that you have done with us in this book.

Sexton Smith

You're more than welcome. I appreciate your giving me the opportunity to have this conversation and to share some of my beliefs because this is what it's all about—developing a deeper understanding of each other so that we may begin to walk in rhythm!

Wright

Today we've been talking with Barbara Sexton Smith. Barbara, thank you for being with us today on *Remarkable Women of Faith*.

About the Author

BARBARA SEXTON SMITH is among the Top Ten Speakers for the International Speakers Network and is a nominee for the 2007 Woman of Achievement Award. She is a distinguished member of the 100 Wise Women for Leadership Louisville and was recently honored by the Kentuckian Girl Scouts during their 95th Birthday Celebration! Barbara was named the 2003 Community Angel by *Today's Woman*. She and her husband, Lacey, received the 2006 McDaniel Bluitt Hope Award for instilling hope in the hearts of so many young people.

Barbara Sexton Smith
Quick Think Seminars
711 West Main Street
Louisville, KY 40202
Phone: 502.583.0467
E-mail: barbara@barbarasextonsmith.com
www.barbarasextonsmith.com

Chapter 3

AMBERLY NEESE

THE INTERVIEW

David Wright (Wright)
Amberly Neese is a remarkable woman of faith indeed! As a busy author and speaker, she has encouraged audiences with her humor and candor. She has been featured in works by Starburst, Standard, and Gospel Light Publishers. She also wrote two devotionals, *Fragrance of Faith* and *Treasure of Trust*.

Amberly earned her master's degree from Biola University in May 1999. In addition, Amberly serves as a professor at two universities in their Masters of Education departments.

Amberly married Scott Neese in 1992. He serves as a pastor in California. They have a daughter, Judah Catherine, and a son, Josiah Caleb.

Amberly, welcome to *Remarkable Women of Faith*.

Amberly Neese (Neese)
Thank you, sir. Thank you indeed.

Wright
How would you define the term "remarkable woman of faith"?

Neese
That is a daunting question. When my friend, Jennifer, called me and told me there is a book project she thought would be perfect for me titled *Remarkable Women of Faith*, I didn't know whether to burst into tears in humility or to just give her a big hug. It was so wonderful that someone would think of me in that light.

With that said, I would like to discuss what it means to have remarkable faith. For me, faith is when a person clearly and decisively chooses to abide and trust in God. How is remarkable faith manifested? Well, when I think of remarkable, I think of diamonds. They gleam and glitter, but when jewelers put on their loupes to look more closely, they see the natural flaws that occurred in the creation of the diamond. The flaws separate diamonds from imitations.

We are much like diamonds, although our flaws were created by past experiences and choices. To have remarkable faith is to be willing to be completely vulnerable to God—to show Him our flaws and then to ask Him to take those flaws and help us find a way to use them to help others. His light can be refracted in those areas of past experiences and choices to create a beautiful, valuable gem.

Wright
From what spiritual lineage did you come and how did it shape your faith?

Neese
I am the daughter of a woman who was culturally Catholic, meaning she upheld Catholic practices but her relationship with God was not really prioritized or modeled as it could have been. My father, on the other hand, graduated from the University of California, Berkley in the late '60s with a degree in Political Science. He dabbled in many faiths, but he taught me how to research and grapple with issues as I found my own path through them. My step-dad was mistreated by a Christian church in his teens, which soured him a little.

They all did their best to support me and celebrate my spiritual journey. When I became a Christian at the age of ten and further pursued God in my late teens, the disappointments and troubles my parents faced in their spiritual journey served me well as I pursued my own spiritual path.

Wright
What life experiences precipitated a hunger for spiritual things?

Neese
Most likely it was the divorce of my parents when I was ten. It was overwhelming for me at the time. I thought for sure my life was over, but of course it wasn't. The experience left me feeling fearful and lonely. My mom's marriage to a new, wonderful man precipitated a move from northern California to Arizona. It meant leaving everyone I knew and loved.

There was a little girl living next door to our new house in Phoenix. Her parents wouldn't let us play together unless I went to church, which in retrospect is not an evangelistic tool I recommend. My parents allowed them to take me to North Phoenix Baptist Church, which is a huge Southern Baptist church in Phoenix.

I listened to the preacher who was an amazing speaker, but was astounded at how he could put fifteen syllables in Jesus' name with his dramatic storytelling. His message of God's love and acceptance really resonated within me. He told the story of God sending His Son to be my friend and the Healer of my wounds. He communicated God's desire for me to celebrate the things happening in my life. That was the message I needed to hear.

Very early on, somebody shared with me a passage from Joshua 1:9, which is still my favorite verse in the Bible. It says, "Do not be afraid and do not be discouraged, the Lord your God will be with you wherever you go." Even at ten years of age, I knew His presence was exactly what I needed—a journey mate, a traveling companion to be always at my side. I needed God. The things that had happened to me needed to rest in the hands of Someone more powerful and more knowledgeable than I was.

Wright
How do trials factor into your spiritual development?

Neese
Our life experiences, for the bad or the good, are essential to the fabric of who we are and our spiritual development.

I taught junior high school for many years in California. We had a yearly field trip to Catalina Island off the coast. From time to time we would snorkel there, which meant swimming in the gorgeous kelp beds. I would watch the movement of the ocean force the kelp to sway back and forth. Imagine my surprise when I learned that without the tide tearing at the kelp, stretching it to its limits, the kelp would die!

That's how I feel about life. When we experience trials in life, we often feel challenged, even overwhelmed or worse. But the truth is that without our trials, we would never develop the strength we need. When the Bible tells us to rejoice in the face of trials it's because the testing of our faith is about perseverance. Perseverance must complete its work so that we may be complete, not lacking in anything. When I am being stretched, I remind myself that God is working in my best interest and I can trust Him. He is saying to me, "I am in charge of this stretching and I have great things planned for you."

Wright

What trials have you faced since becoming a Christian that made an indelible mark?

Neese

My father died at age fifty-one, when I was in my early twenties. Although I was certain God was working in my best interest, at the same time I had been praying that He would save my dad. Instead, he died. That was very hard for me. I didn't blame God, only myself. I told myself that I had caused my father's death through something I had failed to do. Not only did God not abandon me, He began to fill my life with people who had love to offer and wisdom to help sort out my disappointment.

Another trial was my desire to have children. My husband and I will have been married for fifteen years next month, which is really exciting, but for the first nine years of our married life, we had no success in producing children. We tried this and that, even did tests to discover which body part might not be working. We had a miscarriage, which was very devastating. With every baby shower I attended, a part of me seemed to die. I remember saying, "God, if you do not want us to have children, just take away this desire." Again, I was being stretched.

Now, I can say with certainty that God used that time in my life to help draw me closer to Him. In His goodness, because He was faithful to me, He gave me the perspective that allows me to speak about the areas of divorce, death, the miscarriage, and my other trials in a way that most resonates with my audiences. I also have a dimension of empathy that would not have developed without those dark seasons.

Wright

What role does being a female/wife/mother play in your spiritual life?

Neese

Wow, that is an interesting question. I know that some churches celebrate women and some feel that women have only very limited roles. Trying to find my place in that was challenging early in my college years, but no more. I'm certain that God did not make any mistakes when he gave me ovaries. I trust that He makes great decisions. Who I am is female, a wife, and a mother. That is how God created me and it is amazing.

I love that He gave me the opportunity to choose a man who brings out the best in me, just as I bring out the best in him. My husband is an incredible role model and every day I feel very blessed to be Mrs. Matthew Scott Neese. He's also a human being. Ask two imperfect people to spend the rest of their lives together and there's sure to be some friction. Learning to love and accept my husband for who he is has been a catalyst in my growth as a person.

I also love being a mom. Raising my kids has been both empowering and humbling. They serve as my mirror, manifesting my flaws for me to see and accept. It is also delightful to watch them make choices that honor God. Their stories serve as great fodder for speaking anecdotes.

Wright

What role does humor play in your spiritual life?

Neese

When I first started on my spiritual journey, I confused being serious *about* my faith with being serious *in* my faith. The more I grew, and continue to grow, the more convinced I am that God is a giggler. I believe He knows just how powerful and healing laughter and humor are. He enjoys His people—He enjoys our humor, He enjoys fellowshipping with us. I think that the gift of humor is one of the most powerful gifts He has given me.

I also think I make more progress in my spiritual journey when I'm not overly serious about it. That's not to say that I'm casual about my faith. Instead, in laughter I find myself free and empowered to examine my flaws and foibles. I take Him seriously, but have learned to not do likewise with myself! I love when Jesus says, "I am come that they might have life, and that they might have it more abundantly" (John 10:10 KJV). As far as I am concerned, living life "more abundantly"—to the fullest—must include laughter and humor.

Laughter also serves to break down a lot of barriers. It helps me connect with my audiences. Once we're connected, explaining joy in Christ is easy.

Wright

What disciplines or practices help you continue on your spiritual quest?

Neese

There are so many. Delving into the Bible and mentoring and meeting with others to discuss spiritual things is important. Church attendance, listening to teachers, being rigorous with my exercising, they are also all part of it.

But I would have to say that my greatest discipline is my speaking ministries. My speaking makes me study the Word—the Bible. It makes me study the Bible critically because I am preparing to speak to an audience. Because I allow those who engage me to choose the topic for my presentations, I am free to explore all sorts of things, which is really fabulous. Also, I'm finally certain that when I'm speaking I'm always at the right place in the universe.

There is a scene in the movie *Chariots of Fire* where the character, Eric Little, is asked why he runs. His answer is, "When I run I feel God's pleasure." That is how I feel about my speaking ministries. It may be my mouth moving on stage, but it is His pleasure I feel as the words leave me. I am so thankful and honored that He is able to use me in my speaking ministries.

I want to say to everyone who is not enjoying life or doing the things that make them passionate, "Run or speak or scuba dive or whatever it is that makes your heart beat fast," because God wants great things for us. Yes, we have to pay the bills, but we will honor God, feel His pleasure, and hear His words more completely if we do those things to which we are drawn.

Wright

How would you best describe your relationship with God?

Neese

Oh, I would describe it as a work in progress. I feel like one of those construction signs that say: "Please excuse our mess, we are in the process of creating something great." I know God is making something beautiful in me. I trust Him. He can see the blueprint of all the work that yet needs to be done. Again, even though the process may not feel comfortable, I am thankful that my relationship with God is one of trust and allowing Him to do good work.

I also love that God wants to be personal with us. If we truly believe God knows us and knows our inner thoughts, then how silly it is to try to hide them and not be candid with Him. My mother once mentioned that a friend of hers felt it wasn't okay to be angry with God. I replied that it wasn't okay to *stay* angry at God. He loves us enough to love us where we are and loves us enough to not allow us to stay angry. He is a big boy—He is Creator of the universe. He molded the Grand Canyon. He can certainly take the ranting of a thirty-seven-year-old woman when she is disappointed or frustrated. So, my relationship with God is very candid. He honors me with being candid back.

I hear Him speak through the words of friends, through the Bible, and through life experiences. God and I have a great working relationship. In Philippians 1:6 I read, "We can be confident in this, that He who began a good work in us will be faithful to carry it on to completion, until the day of Christ Jesus." I am working on being totally confident that He who began that good work—He who started that construction in me—will carry it on to completion. The more I grow, the more I trust, the more I am blessed.

About the Author

AMBERLY NEESE is a woman of remarkable faith and joy. As a busy author and speaker, she has encouraged audiences with her humor and candor. She has been featured in works by Starburst, Standard, and Gospel Light Publishers. She also wrote two devotionals, *Fragrance of Faith* and *Treasure of Trust*.

Amberly earned her master's degree from Biola University in 1999. She now serves as a professor at two universities in their Masters of Education departments.

Amberly married Scott Neese in 1992. He serves as pastor in Bakersfield, California. They have a daughter, Judah Catherine, and a son, Josiah Caleb.

Amberly Neese
Mouthpeace Ministries
5416 Pacer Valley Ct.
Bakersfield, CA 93313
Phone: 661.747.6240
E-mail: mouthpeace1@sbcglobal.net
www.mouthpeace.us

Chapter 4

JENNIFER O'NEILL

THE INTERVIEW

David E. Wright (Wright)
Today we're talking with Jennifer O'Neill. She is an internationally acclaimed actress, film and television star, successful spokeswoman, composer, author, artist, proud mother of three, and (at the time of this interview) grandmother of four. Jennifer O'Neill has already accomplished enough for a lifetime. She began her international modeling career at the age of fifteen, after her family moved to New York from her native home of Rio de Janeiro, Brazil. Her career in the entertainment industry boasts many feature films including the classic *Summer of '42*, numerous television movies, and three television series. In addition, Jennifer held a thirty-year position as spokeswomen for Cover Girl Cosmetics. Following the success of her biography, *Surviving Myself,* Jennifer has written other books including, *From Fallen to Forgiven, You're Not Alone, A Fall Together, A Winter of Wonders,* and *A Late Spring Frost.* She also wrote a novel that was published by *Campus Crusade* titled, *Lifesavers.* She has served on the Board of Media Fellowship International.
 Jennifer, welcome to *Remarkable Women of Faith.*

Jennifer O'Neill (O'Neill)
Thank you so much, David, it's my pleasure to be here.

Wright
All of us at Insight Publishing are excited about this project, Jennifer. To a person, all of us have been shaped by one or more remarkable woman—women such as our mother, a certain teacher, or a mentor. Although our authors won't admit it, we believe that they are remarkable women in their own right. I'm eager to explore this subject with you, but before we get down to the nitty-gritty, would you tell our readers what you've been up to lately?

O'Neill
David, sometimes when you ask for God's will in your life, you'd better put your seatbelt on. Often you find yourself doing things you never would have imagined. I have been so blessed since I wrote my first book, to have traveled on the speaking circuit. I have spoken to large groups with other women of faith—sometimes thirty thousand at a clip.

In 2002 I was the National Spokesperson for *Silent No More*, an awareness campaign, which deals with the issue of abortion and healing of abortion through God's grace. The campaign is fantastic and has made such a difference in the lives of women and families, healing through the grace of God.

I have also been blessed to have a platform to discuss various negative issues in my life that God has turned into positives. As it says in His Word, *"He will turn all things for good to those who love Him."* There are certain things and events that I have experienced in my life that have afforded me a platform to share some really wonderful news about God's grace and restoration. My speaking engagements take me to schools, colleges, the Senate and Congress, as well as to churches everywhere. I'm able to address the tough issues of teen suicide, abortion, and sexual abuse. (My daughter was sexually abused and she asked me to address that issue.) I also address domestic violence, depression, and other tough issues that many people experience. Very few of us side-step hard issues in life.

The good news is that God wants us healed, whole, existing in an enlightened state, and released though forgiveness and grace. It's there for all of us to have if we ask for it. It's all in Gods Word.

Traveling around the country speaking to women about women's issues, I see so many women who come up after I speak, usually in a flood of tears confessing an abortion they had or that they've been sexually abused or they're having difficulties with depression. I peel like an onion and let them know that they're not alone about certain issues. I love women. These are bright, vibrant, amazing women who in some areas of their lives are stuck in a shameful, guilty, fearful part of their past. None of those things are of the Lord and He is well capable and willing to heal us, if we bring those issues to Him.

Some time ago I decided to do a syndicated television series for women so that we can reach more women with this good news of what God offers us. It is titled, *Living Forever... More. Living Forever... More* is a half-hour, syndicated series in a one-hour Network special. At this time it appears as though it will not only be on syndicated television channels, but also on a new advanced channel on the Web. We hope to be reaching millions of women through this project.

We plan to film a women's retreat with fantastic speakers. All the women in the first retreat are leaders in their own right. Each of these women come from different denominations, are different ages, and are coming together to edify each other and lift each other up, share information, listen to our speakers, have a concert, and laugh and cry.

There are fun segments as well—it's not all about hard healing. It's about sharing, getting back to hospitality, and cooking. It's just going to be an absolute celebration of women. It is an encouragement to women to deal with some of those tough issues so they can be all that they can be in Christ. Since you can't give what you don't have, we want to give information they need because God wants to help women be released from their hard issues.

Wright

That sounds great. Jennifer, I know movie stars grow up like the rest of us "normal" people, and you are the person you are today because of the women who loved you as a young person. Will you tell us about the remarkable women in your life and perhaps how they influenced you in your early years?

O'Neill

That is such a wonderful question. I'd love to start with my mom. I've had my times, as many women do, with some of the areas we want to smooth out between mom and daughter. We seem to go through various cycles. I always asked the women on my television show this question, "Is it a compliment when somebody says you're just like your mom, or is it an insult?"

I have gleaned so much wonderful information and style from my mom. She is a lady to the nth degree. She was born in London. She's an extremely loyal, reliable, beautiful, elegant individual. If I have any twirl with a pen or the written word it's probably because she insisted that I develop my skills in communication. That was a great gift. I love her dearly.

Then there was my Aunt Eleanor, who I must say, in many ways I was, during certain stages of my life, closer to than to my mom because she was more playful. I missed that with my mom. Ellie would play cards with me or go out and help me with my little rock garden. She seemed to embrace my love of animals, which was foreign to my parents because they didn't know it growing up. She encouraged me. She had a piano and she encouraged me to play the piano and write and be expressive.

I remember as a young girl, when my parents would have a party, I would go twirling into the middle of the party dancing and leaping about. Ellie would always applaud and encourage my behavior. I don't know how it was received by anyone else, but just pleasing my aunt was fine. She encouraged me to express myself and upon her death, she left me her piano, which I've had with me for so many years. She also was a very godly woman. Although I didn't have any formal upbringing in the church, Ellie personified Christ who lived in her. If she had any influence, at the top of the list of the influences, I would say that she inspired me to be like her in that sense.

What was it in her that was different? What was it that gave her patience that no one else seemed to have, a compassion that no one else seemed to have? She had a heart just as big as the outdoors. When I came, very late in my life, to my belief and faith in Jesus Christ, I recognized that's what she gave me. She was just a faithful, godly, wonderful woman who planted in me a seed of her presence and her personality and her heart that I desired and aspired to.

I remember another lady, Mrs. Leone. I still remember her name. I think she was my fifth grade teacher. Some of the events in my life were born of the fact that I felt somewhat invisible and unlovable for various reasons. Early on I thought I needed to earn love. I didn't realize it was a free gift and unconditional. I didn't know because I didn't have my faith. I thought that if I got straight A's in school that my parents would love me and I would get their attention. It's a very basic and interesting view.

If we see bruises on a child's face or they're not fed, we know they're an SOS there and they need help. Many times the bruises that we carry through life through a negative impression are on our hearts. You can't see them, but you see the result of them—the hurt.

Well, with all that said, I was just determined to get straight A's in school, and in those days there were about fourteen marks. I had straight A's for all the three-year terms, except one B in spelling. In fact, I can't spell to this day. But this lady—this wonderful teacher—gave me an A in spelling. She wrote a note to my parents and said, "It's not that I'm saying that Jennifer's spelling is up to snuff and I would give an A for her actual talent in that area, but I've never seen any person want straight A's more than Jennifer does. So I'm going to give her an A for effort." That was wonderful because she instilled in me the idea to forge ahead.

If you're not naturally gifted in a certain area but you want to conquer that area—you want to become accepted for whatever reason—keep trying, keep going. If nothing else, you will be rewarded or recognized for your effort. Never give up. That's what she taught me.

Wright

She would be proud today to know that you've become a well-read person and also an author.

O'Neill

Thank God for spell-check!

Wright

Were there any famous women authors or public figures who influenced you as a young person or later in your life?

O'Neill

Yes, Margaret Meade. I was attending private school in New York and believe it or not, she came for an assembly meeting. She was such a great anthropologist. That ignited an interest in me about the world.

I never meet Helen Keller, but she was certainly a positive influence. There are so many women, if you start going through history. It's rather endless.

Wright

I probably should have asked this earlier in the interview, but I've saved the question until now for a specific reason. What do you think makes a woman remarkable?

O'Neill

Women are remarkable in such a wide variety of areas because they have such an array of talents. I would say it would be their ability to accept others in an inspirational and nurturing fashion. Whether an artist or a mother, women have a communication and caring level in them that is unique only to women. It is different than men. I think those that excel remain in touch with those parts of their femininity and are extremely effective. Those are extraordinary women to me—remarkable women are women who have not lost the idea that they're women. They do not have to conquer something.

Here's an analogy. My ex-husband used to be a rodeo cowboy. When I train a horse, my desire is to become a partner with that horse. It's an extraordinary match when it's right—when you're flying through the air (hopefully with the greatest of ease). That big animal desires to please you, is guided by just the lightest touch of your finger or your leg. It's just wonderfully elegant. My ex-husband would want to conquer the horse. He would want to "break" the horse. There's a difference. So he used to laugh at me and say, "You take ten times longer to break that horse than I do." But that was my approach.

What I admire about women is there is that soft touch, that incredible effectiveness, never losing their gentle touch.

Wright

Based on your description, which I agree with whole heartedly, many people would consider Jennifer O'Neill a remarkable woman. And I know you're not looking for a compliment.

O'Neill

I'm just trying to learn.

Wright

I know you to be a very humble person, but I would like to pursue some of the circumstances in your life that caused you to stretch and to grow, to endure and to overcome. I know our readers would be encouraged. If you don't mind, would you relate a story or two about how you have overcome some of the challenges in your life?

O'Neill

Well, for a very long time I wasn't overcoming very well. I almost died three times. I was shot and I had nine miscarriages along the way to having my three children. I was bumping into life very hard. I also broke my neck and back riding horses. But that's why I wrote my first book, *Surviving Myself,* because quite often we get in our own way. Those stumbling blocks in life—those tough ones in my case, such as being able to address my abortion as so many others who have had abortions—carried through my life and that negative feeling grew.

On the other side was the fame and fortune, traveling the world, working in Paris at age fifteen by myself, and all that a life in the public and fast lane could bring. During all that I had this hole in my heart. When I said earlier that God turns all things for good, He has used all those hard times for me to be able to say experience overrides theory.

When I started to really come into my own, my life wasn't a runaway train. I always had enormous drive. I like that about myself, but I realize now as I look back that it had a bit of frenetic tilt to it. I was tenacious on one hand and very shy on the other. What put it all together for me was my faith. It had to start with some very deep healing of those areas and accepting that someone, namely God, could actually love me and care about me, that He knew every hair on my head. He knew me before the creation of time and He knit me together in my mother's womb. He had a plan for me that was bigger than anything I could ever imagine. So talk about inspiration, that's a pretty exciting release. Not only did I receive eternal life, but it took me a good ten years to begin to accept what has always been a free gift from Christ—His love and His protection. The Holy Spirit isn't just a hospital, He's an army to engage. I had to accept that I could achieve anything that He set me on a path to do.

When I finally gave up "me" and realized that if I had any talents they were gifts from God, I wanted to use them for His glory. It was as if a floodgate had opened. We're all a work in progress, but I can begin to see the light at the end of the tunnel, and it's *not* a train! I saw how He used my movies so I'd know how to put together the *Living Forever* television series to edify women and share the good news.

Anything that I do I just give all the glory and honor to God because I wouldn't be here if I hadn't found Him. I had to stop looking down at all the stumbling blocks that I'd put in front of me or others had.

At the end of the day we're all responsible for everything we think, say, and do. When I finally got over myself—a daily laying down of bad tendencies and just asking God to come and fill me up with the Holy Spirit and be available to Him—my life just transformed. I am excited every day. Words come out of my mouth that are from the Word, *"This is the day that the Lord has made and I will be glad in it."* A lot of the tortures that I went through were self-inflicted. It's changing your mind about how you perceive reality.

I have had a good marriage. My husband is a godly man. He's not perfect, I'm not perfect, but he has not been placed on the earth to make me happy. My happiness, my fulfillment, my satisfaction, and my peace come from my relationship with Jesus. I take advantage, if you will, of all His incredible offers to me, like dying on the cross for my sins. I accepted that finally—it's for all my sins. It's for everyone's sins.

When I finally accepted that I wasn't bound to my past through regrets, shame, pain, and all those secret places that we're so good at hiding and shoving under the carpet, I realized the truth really does make you free. When I accepted His grace, I started to heal. Now, I'm a better mom, I'm a better wife. I go into those relationships thinking what can I do for my husband and then I give him to God. I was a control freak because I was afraid of rejection and hurt, most of which I had invited into my life myself through lack of discernment and not having a solid foundation. All of that is changing and it's exciting for me.

Wright

I can understand why it would take you years. When you consider grace, forgiveness, eternal life, it's almost so overwhelming that it seems too good to be true.

O'Neill

Exactly, but it *isn't* too good to be true—God is true. I came to my faith at thirty-eight and it took some time before I really allowed myself to accept His grace.

Wright

Today's modern women must deal with countless challenges from the workplace and at home. In your opinion, what are two or three of the most critical issues facing women today and what advice would you offer women regarding these issues?

O'Neill

In my show I call it "the balancing act." Today, women's plates are so full. You just said it in the question. In the workplace or at home, we're torn. There's not a better job or a more important job than raising children and being a good wife and mom. Yet, we want to expand our territories and be all we can be. It's that balancing act that quite often seems to be a runaway train. And in its wake, what's left are broken relationships.

I also say in my show, "You turn around in bed and you look at your husband and say, 'Who are you and how did you get here?' " I think our relationships suffer because of the complexities of life. Also, we lose the knack of getting along in our marital relationships. I can only speak of this because I'm the worst offender. I finally began trying to figure it out. As I said before, I focus on changing myself and letting God do a work in my husband. Communication is the key and the fact that there are really no surprises.

Married women reach a point in their marriage when they'll say, "I don't recognize you," or "How did I ever get involved with you?" The fact of the matter is that most of the problems we have after the perfect dating stage were evident in the beginning, but we just choose not to look at the problems or we whitewash them thinking everything will be fine. Then we deal with them in our relationship later. I think those are difficult areas to balance.

One thing that might be off the question but I'd like to bring up is, I think women are confused. I think men and women have become confused about their roles over the last generation. It does not bode well for solid family living. I see the desire of families to get back to that balance. We were designed a certain way. Again, I can speak of this because I was always an independent woman who made a very good living and had a lot of exposure in life.

Celebrity, if you will, is not about getting a table at a restaurant, but for me, it allows me to have a platform for God's Word. During those years of imbalance, I didn't choose men who were terribly dynamic. Maybe it was a protective thing on my part. So I was in the driver's seat, financially and power wise. I don't say that with any kind of intent other than to state a fact. I was a very emotionally needy individual. That's not an attractive picture.

When I started to come into my faith and really understand the Word of God and the authority of His ultimate Word on how He designed us to be as man and wife, I realized that's how it has to work. We wives need to acquiesce to our husband as a man. That's difficult for women sometimes because their men, quite often, are not acting like God describes in the Bible a man (husband) should act. There's nothing wrong to listening to a man who, according to the Bible, would lay his life down for his wife and treat her like Jesus treats the church. Men love to be there, but when wives want to open our own door and make our own decisions, that strips our husbands of that. At the same time it strips us of that wonderful feeling of being able to fall into our husband's arms and feel safe and protected yet still have our own identity. He would want us to be the best we can be. I think that's gotten very confusing.

Women have confused the issues. The nth degree is the subject that I talk about all the time, such as abortion, where somehow society has managed to convince women that they have lost some inalienable right if they don't have the right to kill their own child. Something is terribly wrong with what one would call independence. By the way, the early feminists were all pro-life, which is so interesting to me. They were all pro-life. They just wanted the right to vote and they wanted the right to own their own property. They did not want a right to abort their children. So there's been a big mix-up, I think, in the feminist movement. The roles are confused and I think it's caused a lot of problems.

Wright

I think it confuses men. I know I'm confused by the confusion. It doesn't take a rocket scientist to figure out that we're different. I don't understand the unisex thought that all of us should be the same.

O'Neill

It's so wrong and it's led the family and society down a very slippery slope. It doesn't work. I love to tell this to kids when I go to schools and talk about abstinence. Again, I'm the worst offender, but I also tell people that God is so gracious. I remind people—I don't tell them—that God is so gracious with us that when that negative tape, that little voice says, "You're not worthy. You're not lovable. Who are you to stand up and talk to anybody?" (I hear that every morning when I get up and then I just rebuke it). God has given us example after example of people He's used in a powerful way, people who were just as imperfect as we are. Moses was a murderer and stuttered, and didn't want the job. The Apostle Paul called himself the worst offender—at one time he was killing Christians. Peter denied Christ. Whenever I feel that I'm infallible I just remember Peter. We need God's grace every step of the way. I think that we can all be used in a way that we cannot even imagine if we would allow Him to work in us.

Back to your question, I was talking about the kids. I get to go to schools and talk about abstinence. I give them this illustration, David, I tell them to just think for a moment that we are God's design and when God refers to being abstinent until marriage, do you have any idea why, and what the thinking is behind that? It is because He loves us. If you believe that God created us, out of all of His creations—animals and plants, etc.—only people are designed anatomically to face each other when they make love. What would that be about? It is about intimacy and trust and looking into each other's eyes. What is trust but commitment? You can't trust somebody not to leave if they are not committed. What is commitment but marriage? God designed us to be with one another in a trusting, committed fashion. Read the Song of Solomon. God designed sex, but He designed it to be enjoyed under circumstances that won't hurt us. Today, I see healing happening and relationships coming together again. By getting in the right relationship with God, the trickle-down effect is wonderful as we're starting to heal.

Wright

Jennifer, you know, you're one of my favorite people. I just love to talk with you. I always want to go on and on forever. I always learn so much when I talk with you.

When you were describing your mother I was thinking, she's describing herself because you are certainly a class act.

O'Neill

Then just a little bit of her wonder rubbed off on me, and I thank her.

Wright

Today we have been talking with Jennifer O'Neill. It's been my sincere pleasure to speak with her. She's a television and film star, but to those who know her well, she is much, much more.

Jennifer, thank you so much for sharing your heart and soul with our readers today.

O'Neill

It's such a pleasure for me to be a part of this project. I will pray God's blessings on it because women need to read about other wonderful women. We're all wonderful and we're all wonderfully made. It's just a super project!

JENNIFER O'NEILL is by far one of the world's most beautiful Hollywood film stars of all time. She started her international modeling career at the age of fifteen. She then became a film star in some of Hollywood's most bankable films like *Rio Lobo* (with John Wayne) and the award-winning classic film *The Summer of '42* (this movie made Jennifer a household name). Jennifer held a thirty-year position as spokeswomen for Cover Girl Cosmetics. Jennifer is also an animal activist, she races, trains, and breeds show horses, and is an advocate for charitable causes like the American Cancer Society and women's issues. Jennifer's career has been a dream come true, but her life was a nightmare of broken marriages, near death experiences, emptiness, abuse, and even her daughter being sexually abused by one of O'Neill's husbands. She turned her life around by becoming a born-again Christian and now ministers to hurting people worldwide through seminars and her books. Jennifer's books have won critical acclaim and her seminars are attended by millions. Jennifer is an amazing lady, a mother of three children and a grandmother. She's a survivor and has become a role model to all who hear her story.

Jennifer O'Neill
Jennifer O'Neill Ministries
Leah Persell, Executive Assistant
1811 Beech Ave.
Nashville, TN 37203
Phone: 615.463.3126
Fax: 615.463.3032
E-mail: jenniferoneill@bellsouth.net

Chapter 5

YVONNE CONTE

THE INTERVIEW

David Wright (Wright)
Today we're talking with Yvonne Conte. Yvonne is a highly gifted storyteller with a comedic edge and a powerful message about life. She is a member of the National Speakers Association, author of five books, and she holds a degree in communication. Yvonne has a unique niche as an ordinary woman overcoming adversity. She has faced personal challenges, major career changes, death, illness, and single parenthood with unshakable optimism, deep faith, and a sense of humor. She conveys a love for the Lord that is contagious. Her straightforward, uplifting style sets a positive tone for any conference. Her closing talks leave audiences spellbound and looking at life from a new perspective. Her charismatic presence inspires audiences to take action and achieve greatness in life personally and professionally. She is a partner at Syracuse Vineyard, she is a motivational humorist, author, mother, and most recently she became a grandmother!

This book is called *Remarkable Women of Faith*, so what makes you a remarkable woman of faith, Yvonne?

Yvonne Conte (Conte)
I'm really an average everyday woman who just hooked up with an inexhaustible and remarkable God. I think that when you belong to an incredible all-powerful God, and you're linked up with Jesus and the Holy Spirit, it's pretty easy to feel like a remarkable woman of faith. I have a strong faith and I lean on that faith when I need it, which is every day.

Wright
Will you describe your relationship with the Lord?

Conte
My relationship with the Lord is like any relationship and that means active communication. When you have a relationship with anyone it's all about communication. I communicate with Him every day in prayer, which means being able to tell Him exactly what's on my mind and hearing Him and understanding His response. When you have that kind of relationship with anybody and you're able to talk about just about anything at any time, well, that's how I feel about the Lord. I can talk to Him anytime I want and that's quite a wonderful relationship. He's with me in everything I do and in everything I say.

I guess the difference is that now I love Jesus and I want to obey Him because I love Him and I want to please Him. When I was a little girl I remember I wanted to be a good person. I wanted to obey the Ten Commandments. I wanted to go to heaven. I wanted to please my mom and dad. That kind of obedience really has nothing to do with faith or relationships. Now it's a whole different thing. I do what I feel is the right thing because I love the Lord, not because I want to please someone here on earth.

Wright
Was there a specific moment when you actually found your faith in Jesus and made a commitment?

Conte
I don't have a story of a particular time when fantastic faith hit me in the head with a bulldozer like some people do, but what I do have is a very long, drawn out period of time when the Lord opened my eyes.

When I was a little girl I used to think that God was trying to speak to me. I was a little afraid to tell anybody. I remember especially that our street backed up to a very high hill that overlooked a busy highway. I used to go there because the wind was always blowing and that sound blocked out the sound of the traffic. It was a great place for me to really connect with God. I sat there a lot when I was a kid on that little hill. I remember thinking that He had an important job for me. I wasn't sure what that job was but I felt like I really had a connection with the Lord back then.

I went to a Catholic school; in fact I went to an all girls' Catholic boarding school. I remember telling Sister Paul (I think it was in the seventh grade) that I wanted to be a nun and I thought that Jesus was calling me. Her exact words were, "Honey, you would make a better mother than you would a nun." She discouraged me from entering the convent.

I was reprimanded constantly when I was in that school. Some of it was for asking too many questions in religion class. It wasn't that I didn't believe what they were teaching, I just wanted to understand it. If it didn't make sense to me I kept questioning it and I was always in trouble. I think I was always being tugged that way.

I married a Methodist man. I remember that I would get up early and go to Mass at eight in the morning, then I would run down the street and go to the Methodist church at eleven because I wanted to make sure I hit them both. I wasn't sure which one was the right place. It was like "religious insurance."

It was in the Methodist church where I really learned about faith. We attended a small church and they needed me because there were not that many adults in the church. I was a Sunday school teacher, a member of the choir, and of the ladies group. They pulled me into every corner of the church and because of that I learned a lot. I loved it. I started my own faith search and read everything I could get my hands on to try to figure out where it was that God wanted me to be. The Methodist church was a real important part of my faith walk.

Wright

I'm glad to hear that because I'm a Methodist.

Conte

Are you really? I'll bet you can sing then because they can all sing.

Wright

Most of us eat a lot.

Conte

Yes that's true. At those church dinners you've got to save your fork!

Wright

Where do you attend church?

Conte

I go to the Vineyard. The Vineyard is a large community. We have over 600 Vineyard churches in the United States. Actually they are all over the world. It started out in California back in the mid-1970s. We are just a group of people who love the Lord. In this particular Vineyard that I belong to there are so many opportunities to grow in Christ. If you aren't involved in a group other than just on Sunday morning it's because you live under a rock and nobody can get hold of you. There are so many different things you can do and opportunities to grow and to learn and to get involved. It's terrific and I just love it there.

Wright

So it's a service-oriented organization?

Conte

Yes. In fact, we do a lot to serve the community and there are many opportunities to serve. The minute I walked into that building I felt the love of God. I felt the Spirit. I actually went there with my daughter to see a play. I looked at her and I said, "Oh Aubry, can we go to church here next Sunday?" She said, "Sure." I could feel the spirit of the Lord right there in that moment. We went to church that following Sunday and I've been there ever since. I love it.

Wright

Your company, The Humor Advantage, recently celebrated its tenth anniversary. Are you a Christian speaker? What is your background?

Conte

I'm a Christian woman and I'm a motivational speaker, but I don't promote myself as a Christian speaker. I'm a Christian and that's who I am and I do mention my faith, no matter what kind of audience I have. In a world where you have to be politically correct, you wouldn't think I could get away with that but I'm in front of corporate America every week and I always mention that I'm a Christian. I always say, "That's just who I am and it's going to slip out. I know that I have to be politically correct so if you're an atheist or anything like that out there, let me apologize ahead of time and I'll pray for you later." They laugh and I get away with it.

I have a degree in communication, but I don't think that is what qualifies me to speak. I'm a successful national speaker and author because that's what the Lord wants me to do. I really have absolutely no right to do this—I'm not trained. I didn't decide to do this, it just sort of happened for me.

Wright

Why did you choose to be a motivational humorist?

Conte

I was a single mom for years and I sold telephone systems. The company I worked for moved to Florida. We walked in one day and there I was—no job. I lost everything. When you have no income your nest egg turns into a goose egg and soon you don't have enough money to pay your bills. I lost my home. I lost my car. I lost every bit of money I had because it happened during a time when it was difficult to find a job.

My son saw me crying one morning and he said, "Oh my goodness, Mom, what's wrong?"

"It's a terrible thing," I replied, "to be my age and not know what you want to do with your life." I told him that I felt like a complete failure.

It was his idea for me to be a comedian. He said, "You're really funny and you seem to like to make people laugh. You have to be at work all the time so you might as well be doing something that you enjoy."

Of course I dismissed him as an idiot because I thought, "Well, you just can't be a comedian. How are you going to support your family?"

I happened to go to my accountant that same day to try to figure out how I was going to make the last bit of money stretch and he said,

"You've got to get a job. I don't care if you're waiting on tables. You've got to get a job. Have you ever thought of doing stand-up comedy? You're pretty funny."

"Holy mackerel," I thought, "you know, there is somewhere in the Bible that says, out of the mouth of two and three. I'm not good at remembering Scripture but it hit me when the two of them said it the same day.

I started doing stand-up comedy at a small comedy club near my home. Here I was, this Catholic school girl—very principled, I crossed my legs at the ankle, very prim and proper—and I was on this comedy club stage where people were using foul language. It was nothing I was used to in my life. But they would laugh at my comedy. My comedy was crystal clean. It was about life and I kept saying, "Lord, if you don't want me to do this, don't make them laugh." And every night they would just crack up. People would say, "Oh, my mom is just like yours," or something like that. I thought that maybe my mission was to make people laugh for thirty minutes. I decided that if that was what He wanted me to do, then that's what I would do.

God had other plans for me because He kept opening door after door after door to send me in the direction of being a speaker. He had to close a lot of doors before He opened them. I lost everything. I lost almost every material thing I had.

Looking back on it, I think the reason was because I didn't appreciate what I had. I didn't realize it came from God. I bragged about how successful I was selling telephones. I think that the Lord had to take that away because I had all the wrong motives. I didn't appreciate where my gifts were coming from. I would boast about being the Salesperson of the Year. Big deal. I never said, "Thank the Lord for giving me the gift of being a good salesperson." I was on the wrong path and He needed to clean house and get me headed in the right direction. I continued to pray for the ability to know what to do with my life.

My phone rang one day and it was this woman out of the blue who said, "We heard you were hysterical and we would like to have you come and speak for our group." I thought she wanted me to do stand-up so I got my pencil out and was going to write the date down. During the course of our conversation I realized that she wanted me to speak to her business group about the benefits of humor. I thought, "What a great idea!" I'd been in corporate America and I knew they needed that. I never told her I was a comedian. She thought I was a speaker and I just let her think that. This was close to twelve years ago. It has been amazing. It's hysterical because I had no experience, no knowledge on the subject, no money, and no clients; but from this one woman my business has grown year after year after year. We're headed to our biggest year yet coming up and it's just amazing.

Wright

You have worked almost twelve years now, speaking to some of the most prestigious companies in America. You have written and published five books, you're president of a thriving speakers' bureau. Why do you think you have been so successful?

Conte

I think it's having faith. I had faith that this is the path the Lord wanted me to take and I just walked through the doors He opened. I share my story on the podium and I just hope that somebody out there hears that the way to pure happiness and joy is knowing the Lord, loving the Lord, and being grateful for all those things He gives us. I really think that's how I've been successful.

When I started to give Him the credit for my success, my success just continued to multiply. I don't have to work hard—it just happens. I know that some people out there might not understand this but that is exactly how it has worked for me.

Wright

Will you tell us what having the "humor advantage" is about? Do you think it's easier to be joyful when you are a Christian?

Conte

Absolutely. First of all, having the humor advantage is having the ability to handle all the difficulties life hands us just by changing the way you look at life, by having a different perspective on life. It offers the opportunity for us to see the humor in the pain and live your life in a joyful way.

I wish that for everyone but I don't really understand how people can live that way if they don't know the Lord. I think He is your tour guide through life. You lean on Him. Can you imagine going through life with no guidance? I don't know how people do that. Having Him with me every step of the way is what keeps everything in perspective. You look at life differently. The little stuff really doesn't matter. You don't worry and stress over things because you know He's always going to be there—every disappointment, every slip, every failure—

He's going to be right there. Those things will build your character and strengthen you and help you to grow in the Lord too.

Wright

Life isn't perfect so how can we live a life of joy when we have problems?

Conte

We do have problems; they are a part of life. No matter how many blessings we have in our life—we are blessed daily—we will still have problems. There is always something: there are health issues, family issues, financial difficulties, or everyday stuff like yard work that needs attention, whatever it might be. That's what makes life challenging and interesting. Problems and hard work offer us wonderful opportunities to grow and to change.

I think we can be relatively happy here on earth but I don't really think that's our goal. I don't think our goal is just to be happy. Our goal should be to grow in character and I don't think you can do that unless you have difficulties to go through. Our goal should be to be more like Christ. When you're able to laugh in the face of your difficulty, you know that you've grown and learned from the previous one.

I know you're not going to laugh when you get hit by a car. You won't say, "Oh, what a riot!" I totaled my car not too long ago and I didn't say, "Well isn't that great, I wrecked a brand new car." What I did realize was that was the Lord was telling me to slow down. He was telling me that my life was getting to be too fast paced and I needed to slow it down. It was a lesson for me.

I think you have a choice. You can either focus on your purpose—know what your goals are—or you can focus on your problems. People who sit there and whine and complain have that, "Woe is me attitude," which just drives me crazy. They're not focusing on their purpose. Everything isn't perfect and you can just decide to look beyond those imperfections; you'll see the Lord there.

God didn't promise us that we were going to live our whole life with no sorrow and no pain. He did promise us that He would always be there every step of the way and He is. He promised us comfort and life and strength and He'll help us if we just ask Him and recognize that He's there.

Wright

You do presentations every week all over the country. Tell me what it feels like to stand in front of an audience. Do you ever get tired of the same stories or does one blend into another?

Conte

You would think that I would get tired, but I never do. I never get tired of it. When I walk off the stage I always feel 100 percent better than when I walked on—always. I think just hearing the audience laugh pumps me up and energizes me.

Each time I do a presentation it's basically the same but depending on the audience and how they react sometimes comedy gets written right there on the stage while I'm standing there and I'll say to somebody "Write that down, that was good." My audiences energize me; I just love to go to work. My dad said to me one time, "Fall in love with what you're going to do for a living. Find some way to recognize how what you're doing every day positively affects someone else and you'll love to go to work." That's how I feel. I love to go to work. Plus I always learn something too. I believe that being out there and talking with other people is God's way of teaching me to be a better person. It really works that way.

Wright

What do you see as your greatest personal battle or temptation?

Conte

I would say (and I'm embarrassed to have to admit this) that keeping my commitment to spend time every day in the Word is my greatest personal battle. I have my Bible right there and I'll say that I'm going to read every day—I'm going to read a certain amount every day. The day goes by and I get so sidetracked with everyday stuff that I find I've not fulfilled that commitment. Today is a beautiful day. You don't get many beautiful days in December in New York State. So I'll say, "Oh the Lord gave me this beautiful day, He must want me to go out and walk the dog," or, "Wouldn't this be a great day to go Christmas shopping?" So temptations are pretty much everywhere. I love television; I could be on my computer all day; if I walk into the kitchen I could be in there cooking and eating. I really do get quite a few temptations.

Wright

How do you get motivated to write new programs or find new topics for your books? What really drives you to do this sort of work?

Conte

I love it first of all, but I think what drives me and what makes me feel as if what I am doing matters is the moment when I've reached somebody. I usually stand in front of an audience; I don't always get to talk with them afterward. Sometimes, however, some of them will come up to my table afterward. They'll talk to me and say, "I'm so glad I heard what you had to say today because I'm going through that same thing with my daughter." Or I might get an e-mail from someone telling me that something I said made a difference—the person had made a change in his or her life for the better. Then I know that I'm doing the right thing and it motivates me to write new programs and make sure I have better programs to give them each time. You can't imagine the number of people who come up to me and say, "I was so impressed to hear your testimony" or they will tell me how wonderful it was to hear me speak of my faith. Truthfully, I think many people are starving for the Lord.

Wright

How do you feel your faith plays a part in your success and your ability to laugh at life?

Conte

I couldn't get out of bed in the morning if the Lord wasn't there to push me out. He's really a companion. He motivates me. Just knowing that this is what He wants me to do motivates me. Everything I have and everything I am I know I owe to Jesus—I know that. I just feel that He's blessed me and He continues to bless me, so I need to get out there and do His work.

Before I get on stage each time, I pray and say, "Lord, you know who's in my audience and you know what they're dealing with today so you just open up my mouth send these stories out. Make them connect with these folks and make a difference in their life. Just help me to help them to know what is in your will for them." That's my prayer every time I go out there.

Most of my work is storytelling. When I start telling a story I'll say, "I haven't told that story or even thought of it in years, I don't know where that came from. It just came from left field." You know, that is the very story someone will mention. That person will come up to me after the program and tell me that it meant something to him or her. When that happens I know it wasn't me—it was the Lord. The Lord touched them. I just smile and say thank you.

Wright

What a great conversation. I really appreciate your taking all this time with me today to answer all these questions about being a woman of faith. I've learned a lot here today and I'm sure our readers will as well.

Conte

Thank you so much for having me it's been a pleasure.

About the Author

YVONNE CONTE has come a long way from Utica, New York, where she was the second child in her slightly dysfunctional, hysterical immigrant family. She was a guitar-playing folk singer in the sixties with a record album to her credit. A divorced mother of two in the seventies, Yvonne held several jobs. She was a card-carrying union carpenter. She learned how to swing a hammer, hang sheetrock, and balance her checkbook. The telecommunications industry brought her much financial success and she earned the title of Salesperson of the Year five times in the eighties. Yvonne took three decades of experience to the stage in the nineties as a stand-up comic and radio and television personality. She was even a clump of grapes at a bar mitzvah!

Yvonne started out with no formal education in the public speaking industry, but she had persistence and a burning determination to self-education that has distinguished her as an authority on humor, joy, and human potential. Her eagerness to learn and her uncanny ability to turn every obstacle she faced into a learning opportunity helped her rise from a penniless single mom to an award-winning salesperson and later from a banquet and night club comedian to a premier keynote speaker.

Along the way Yvonne faced many failures, losses, and obstacles. There were many times when she wondered why so many bad things were happening in her life. Looking back, she sees God's hands were guiding her through the difficult times. She says it was those difficult times that made her strong, that built her character, and they are what brought her to this moment.

Today, this five-foot, one-inch dynamo is a highly respected, gifted storyteller. Her live presentations generate outstanding audience evaluations: "She's so genuine, easy to understand and relate to; a breath of fresh air; she's hysterical, full of personality; her gripping tale of courage and faith really make you think." Yvonne has been providing her audiences with the Positive Power of Humor since 1995. She gives all credit and praise to our Lord and Savior whose amazing love continues to inspire her to be better, to do more, and to give thanks all day long.

Yvonne Conte
Humor Advantage, Incorporated
4736 Onondaga Blvd., Suite 231
Syracuse, NY 13219
Phone: 315.487.3771
E-mail: smile@yvonneconte.com
www.yvonneconte.com

Chapter 6

DR. RHEBA WASHINGTON-LINDSEY

THE INTERVIEW

David Wright (Wright)
 Today we're talking with Dr. Rheba Washington-Lindsey. Rheba's life has been and continues to be unconditionally led by faith. Her faith has brought her through the turbulent storms of life and her faith continues to bring her solace. She has touched many lives, from those who are homeless to those who are well off. Her remarkable passion to inspire and motivate others has touched the lives of women who are displaced; people who see no purpose in their lives; and, most of all, students from diverse backgrounds who are searching for new knowledge and guidance. Finally, she has motivated, mentored, and inspired teachers from all grade levels. Dr. Washington-Lindsey has spoken to audiences as far away as Africa with her positive message of personal growth. She has written two books: *Teaching in a Culturally Diverse Classroom,* and *Teaching Isn't for Cowards.* Additionally, she is an expert on women's communication. Dr. Washington-Lindsey has five academic degrees in fields ranging from sociology to communication studies. Her enthusiasm earns her a standing ovation—every time.

Dr. Washington-Lindsey, what is it that makes remarkable women of faith radiate?

Dr. Rheba Washington-Lindsey (Washington-Lindsey)

There are numerous characteristics that make remarkable women of faith radiate. I want to discuss three of them.

Let me begin by saying I have been a Christian for a very long time, actually since eighth grade. And, I don't recall one time in which I turned away from the Lord. I love the Lord, trust Him, and believe He died on the cross for me only to rise again for me. My walk with my Savior has not been without its trials, frustrations, and errors on my part. I am thankful that God is forgiving and compassionate and that He loves me. There were times when I walked out on the water without Him as anchor. When the waves got going from a raging storm and I realized that I had stepped out on my own, He was there to shelter me. I had an anchor. When life deals people flowers, they become self-sufficient. But when the going gets tough down the way, they are swept off their feet. Christians—including women of deep faith—who cling to the Lord can weather the fiercest storms of adversity that life places before them. He is always with them. God has never promised to keep us from storms, but to keep us through them. I remember affirming, "He is my refuge and my fortress: my God; in Him will I trust" (Psalm 91:12 KJV).

First, do you remember the story of Mary and Martha? Martha was busy preparing for Jesus' visit while Mary was already sitting at His feet; she didn't bother to help prepare the meal. Isn't Martha just like many women? There are women who try to do two or three things at one time. Multitasking—trying to wear many hats—can sometimes become draining on us mentally, physically, and spiritually. Women by nature are nurturers and we try hard to please. It becomes difficult to radiate for Jesus when we are not at our best. *But,* a remarkable woman of faith calls out to God for provision of His strength to do His work. Matthew 6:33 says it so well, "Seek ye first the kingdom of God and His righteousness . . ." (KJV). That means putting God before each day and seeking His will for your day; then everything will fall in place.

When women go to God on a daily basis they give their schedule to Him and ask Him to order their footsteps lest they fall along the way (see Psalm 119:133). Remarkable women of faith don't try to do everything. They not only go to God early in the morning but then they also wait for Him to speak.

Women are made for the long haul (if we don't die sooner.) This is an extraordinary woman. God is not looking for super heroes, just women who are willing to radiate for Him. When I try to do too much, everything starts to suffer in my life—my walk with the Lord, my relationship with other people, my productivity, and my effectiveness for the Lord; even my physical stamina suffers.

Remarkable women of faith develop a more workable routine and include within that time quiet time with the Lord. These moments will be invaluable. It's the time to have a conversation with the Lord. It doesn't have to be long. Tell Him how grateful you are for the favor of His strength so far, the favor He has given you with the people around you. Thank Him for His favor or intervention and thank Him for the continual favor of His presence. Remarkable women of faith sit humbly and quietly listening to their Lord. When a woman this, the *remarkable woman can't help but radiate where she is.*

Second, remarkable women of faith know how to boldly and effectively witness on the job. Many women work in a male-dominated business or in an environment that is without much Christian influence, if any at all. So, remarkable woman of faith use Christ's model. Remember when He approached the woman at the well (John 4:7–42)? Did the Lord approach her by saying "You'd better repent or else"? No, He simply said, "Give me a drink." He made a statement that drew her attention. He made statements that piqued her curiosity, such as, "Whoever drinks of the water I will give shall never thirst." Now who wouldn't want to hear more about that water? Remarkable women look for opportunities to creatively intertwine a situation on the job with one from the Bible.

Third, remarkable women of faith are obedient. I had to go through hard knocks before I learned that obedience to God gives big results in great blessings. I can easily remember a time in my life when I wanted to run with the in-crowd. That meant I might be compromising my Christian lifestyle. But, I wanted to have fun, by whatever means and I figured the Lord would understand.

I went off to college and one night a group of girls and I decided we were going to tiptoe out of the dorm and go for some good time at the local bar, which was located down the hill behind the dorm. I stepped into that bar and a spirit of fear gripped me. As I looked out across a sea of folks drinking and dancing, my hands began to tremble as I clenched them stiffly to my side; my knees buckled to the point that I could hardly stand in my cute high heels. My mouth became dry and tight when I looked at the faces in that gyp joint. My heart raced wildly as my stomach clenched tight. Fear and anger with myself knotted inside of me. I knew intuitively that something was wrong. Anyway, I was determined to prove to my girlfriends that I was up for the fun. What I feared most happened. A fight broke out. Folks were throwing bottles; cans, glasses, and chairs went flying across the room. I ducked under a table, eyed the exit, and crawled out the door. I made it. I ran as fast as a jackrabbit up that hill and all the way back to my dorm room. In fact, I didn't even stop to sign back in at the front desk. I was terrified. I hadn't listened to God because I had wanted to do my thing. I had been faced with the pressure to conform, and thus I compromised the Scripture's express teaching in favor of worldly behavior.

Obeying God involves choices that may result in loss of friendship, hardship, or rejection. Obedience requires courage. Even if the circumstance proves to be a difficult one, I have found that the Lord honors obedience. When I succumbed to peer pressure that night, I didn't understand that the Lord would empower me to do what was right. Making a commitment to obey God is essential in our faith. In fact, faith and obedience are inseparable.

Wright

Where is your faith, Rheba, when the bottom drops out of your life, meaning when you have failures or disappointments?

Washington-Lindsey

I suppose you mean when life deals me a bad hand? It's amazing how some folks breeze through life without despair. They have no major traumas that upset their world, no catastrophes that dare throw their lives into chaos, no irreconcilable losses that darken their days, no dream disappointed. On the other hand there is a mother weeping outside a hospital room where her son lies after being hit by a drunk driver or a teacher in a classroom who gives 100 percent yet is constantly harassed by his or her supervisor. There are parents who have found themselves laboring over a child gone astray. And we can't forget the man or woman who received discouraging news from the doctor.

I must confess that I have had plenty of days when I asked the Lord, "Why is life so unfair?" I would listen to other women talk about the joys of moving up their career ladders, and I would rejoice with them. I would listen to women talk about how loving their spouses were and I would rejoice with them. I would listen to women talk about how well their supervisor treats them and I would rejoice with them. And, then my heart would cry out, "How long, Lord, must I wait until my change comes?" I would grieve in silence and solitude. But as a woman of faith I know that life isn't always fair and I had to develop strategies for dealing with life when it deals me a bad hand.

One day I turned to Psalm 73, written by Asaph. Asaph got my attention because he too felt that the bottom had dropped out of his life. Asaph was very honest with God. He expresses to us his disillusionment with God. There came a time when Asaph had to admit that he felt betrayed, not only by life but by God. Asaph's lens became clouded by personal resentment and confusion. He cried, "Why is this happening to me? I have trusted the God of our fathers. I've tried to remain faithful to my God. I've tried to make good choices. Yet, I'm overwhelmed with trouble while less principled people prosper. It just isn't fair!" Asaph's faith was being challenged by his life experiences. Like Asaph, I felt that my life was defined by scars; some of which I was unable to understand.

Another biblical character that I found encouraging when my life hit rock bottom was Joseph. Joseph shared the same underserved mistreatment; he too didn't understand why. God did give him a glimpse of the future in his visions as a child, but there was nothing he could put his hands on when suffering the many injustices, dark years of slavery, and abandonment.

When life dealt me an unfair hand as it did to Joseph and Asaph, my faith kept me strong. As I journeyed through my trials, Romans 5:3–5 came to me: "And not only so, but we glory in tribulations also: knowing that tribulation worketh patience; and patience, experience; and experience, hope: and hope maketh not ashamed; because the love of God is shed abroad in our hearts by the Holy Ghost which is given unto us" (KJV). I learned that hardships are to be experienced with patience and that I was to rejoice in hope. Now, how is one supposed to rejoice when the bottom is dropping out of one's life? Being joyful was not what I felt like doing. I just missed the entire concept of rejoicing in the midst of trials and longsuffering.

Then I leaned and depended on Romans 8:28: "And we know that all things work together for good to them that love God, to them who are the called according to His purpose" (KJV). God is faithful. All I needed to do was act confidently, stand firmly on God's Word, and believe that His favor was going to "work all the circumstances of my life together for my good."

Like Asaph, I didn't go into the sanctuary during my dark time. Asaph eventually went to the sanctuary—a place for spiritual hiding where hearts are restored and strengthened for the struggles of today and the challenges of tomorrow. Asaph "found restoration when he went into the sanctuary of God." It is there that he found new perspective and understanding. The sanctuary was the church where he went to pray. Eventually I found spiritual renewal through God and returned to the sanctuary.

Through it all I have learned to hold on to faith as a result of 1 Peter 1:6–8: "Wherein ye greatly rejoice, though now for a season, if need be, ye are in heaviness through manifold temptations: that the trial of your faith, being much more precious than of gold that perisheth, though it be tried with fire, might be found unto praise and honor and glory at the appearing of Jesus Christ. Whom having not seen, ye love; in whom, though now ye see him not, yet believing, ye rejoice with joy unspeakable and full of glory" (KJV). This is a remarkable statement. It clearly speaks to me about holding on to faith in the midst of hardships and the importance of rejoicing when life isn't fair.

Further, the Lord continued to minister to me from 1 Peter 1:6–8. It is the Scripture that reads: "... the trial of your faith being much more precious than gold..." Believe me, I did not see my trials as gold. In fact, if anything, I would have wanted some gold. Can you believe that God has blessed me with trials that are equivalent to gold? Being rich? Wow! Today, I wouldn't trade what has been given to me for anything. My trials have made me a faith-wealthy woman.

Finally, he comforted me during my tribulations. The book of 2 Corinthians 1:3–4 says, "Blessed be God, even the Father of our Lord Jesus Christ, the Father of mercies, and the God of all comfort; who comforted us in all our tribulation, that we may be able to comfort them which are in any trouble, by the comfort wherewith we ourselves are comforted of God. For as the sufferings of Christ abound in us, so our consolation also aboundeth by Christ" (KJV). I began to realize that I wasn't walking alone. That the Lord was right there next to me comforting me, drying my weepy eyes, consoling my broken heart, giving me hope in the midst of hopelessness.

Life is not unfair. It's just that when you are going through trials it seems unfair. Sometimes we are in so much tribulation that we are not able to see the roses and the rainbow—both represent hope. When we became Christians, God never promised in His covenant relationship with us that our lives would be perfect. But, He did make many promises; one of those promises is that He would be with us and comfort us.

I don't place my hope in temporal things like the love of money, achievements, materials possessions; that foundation will inevitably crumble. Things of the world do bring me comfort when it comes to fighting the tumultuous storms of life. I need something stronger, something more stable that will help me stand strong.

I know to whom I belong, and in times of trouble or when life doesn't make sense, He wants me to get out of the way so that He can work.

Wright
Where is your faith when God doesn't answer your prayer?

Washington-Lindsey
Well, as any human being, I want it now. I sometimes find myself saying, "I did it my way." There have been plenty of times when I've told the Lord that I couldn't wait any longer. I even tried to find Scriptures that would justify my moving, only to fall hard. Now, years later, I have learned to wait for God's timing, putting my faith in Him.

Sometimes I would ask God if He heard my cry and I would request, "Lord, when are you going to do something about this need?" I would ask, "Lord, have you forgotten about me?" Waiting is truly a test of my patience because I'm often anxious to get the job done, get the situation taken care of, or fix the problem. Therefore, waiting is a challenge for me. Does it create stress? Indeed, most of the time. When I understand that God has heard me and I am assured that He is in control my life, it is less stressful.

Habakkuk 2:3 says, "For the vision is yet for an appointed time . . . though it tarry, wait for it; because it will surely come, it will not tarry." Note the verb "is" and "will" meaning that the answer is in the process of coming.

I'm reminded of David because he too had a dream similar to mine. Recall that David, a shepherd, cared for his father's sheep. He had a desire to do more for God. I'm certain he became discouraged and questioned God's timing, but David waited on the Lord. David didn't complain about tending the sheep, he didn't tell God to hurry up, nor did he lose heart. He knew he had to act on faith and God would move him to the next level in His time.

In my book *Teaching Isn't for Cowards,* I share the story of a time in 2003 when I wanted God to answer my prayers right then, but I needed to wait. I had a supervisor who couldn't stand me. Most of my colleagues warned me of her continual harassing ploys. However, I refused to accept their warnings. They were right. My supervisor would write me up for mundane acts such as forgetting to dot an *i* or cross a *t*. I couldn't sleep, my life was filled with stress; I began suffering emotionally. My doctor put me on medication to help me relax. I didn't like that.

I began praying and begging the Lord to move me to another school and do it as soon as possible. He didn't; and I decided that I would strike out on my own, finding Scriptures to support my move. This caused me to step out of His favor. I tell you, I ran into more brick walls. Moving on my own increased my stress level, when all I needed to do was to be still. The Lord was saying, "This is not the right time." I couldn't understand why He would allow me to be harassed by a nonbeliever. But 2 Corinthians 4:8–9 says, "We are troubled on every side, yet not distressed; we are perplexed, but not in despair; persecuted, but not forsaken; cast down, but not destroyed . . ." (KJV).

I began to pray a prayer based on Isaiah 54:16–17: Lord, I know you are Creator of all things, you are the one who created the blacksmith who fans the coals into flames, and you promised to destroy the work of the devil who creates havoc. I believe that only you are able to grant me your favor of protection, as you have promised that no weapon formed against me shall prosper and that every tongue that accuses me you will refute. I stand on your promises because your promises are part of the covenant relationship I have with you." I would pray this daily before leaving my house.

I also began to pray a prayer based on Ephesians 6:10–18: "Lord I ask that you dress me in your armor as a soldier going into battle. I pray that your favor will dress me with the boldness to stand against the devil by buckling the belt of truth around my waist, placing the breastplate of righteousness covering my breast, my feet fitted with peace, shield of faith in my hand, the helmet of salvation over my head, and I ask that your word would be continually upon my lips as I reverently pray."

Eventually, in 2004, He began to move in His time. First, He moved her from being my supervisor. Was she mad! And every time this supervisor tried to come after me, the Lord would send an angel to intervene. Second, through a chain of Godly events I was able to move to another school. Praise His name!

David, when God is ready to answer your prayers, all the evil forces of darkness will not be able to stand in His way. I began to stay in a spirit of joy and peace as I waited for God to answer my prayers, knowing that God would give me His grace and He would bring my prayers to pass.

I encourage others to "hold on to your faith, the Lord is coming."

Wright
How do you apply faith in your daily life?

Washington-Lindsey
There were plenty of times in my life when I would hate to go to work or I couldn't bear the thought of facing a Monday, not because I didn't like my job, but because I didn't know what the day would hold. I was not excited about Monday; I saw it as the same old humdrum day, and I certainly didn't expect any good to come out of it.

Now my attitude has changed. I walk by faith each and every day, and expect good things out of Mondays. Let me explain this new phenomenon. Before I enter the door of my workplace, I have already put a song on my lips. I make it a point to happily sing a praise song—something that lets the Lord know how thankful I am for this day. When I greet people coming down the hall, they greet me with, "Good morning, Dr. Lindsey," because it is a good morning, no matter if it is raining or snowing it's always a good morning, and a good day. Then they say, "How are you?" my response is, "I'm blessed."

One morning, one of my colleagues totally disagreed with me. I greeted her with, "Good morning, Barbara," (not her real name), and she did not respond; she just grunted something. One week later I greeted her in my same way and this time she set me straight. "Listen," she said, "let me get one thing straight—there's nothing good about this morning or any other morning. I'm in constant pain and I have no reason to be glad about anything."

I believe that everybody ought to greet each day with an attitude of gratefulness and joy even in the midst of pain, trials, or tribulations. I make it a point to approach each day with enthusiasm and expectancy.

Enthusiasm is entering into the workplace and the day with praise, just as Psalm 100:4 reads: "Enter His gates with thanksgiving and into His courts with praise: be thankful unto Him, and bless His name." I want to put *entheos* into place. Entheos is the Greek root word for enthusiasm, formed from *en,* meaning "in" and *theos,* meaning "God" into place. My life is renewed day by day as 2 Corinthians 4:16 states.

I have learned to work by faith and living in the fruits of the spirit: love, joy, peace, patience, kindness, faithfulness, gentleness, and self-control (from Galatians 5:22). I don't work in a perfect place, nor do I work in an extraordinarily special profession. With that in mind, I make enthusiasm a choice. I practice the principle of Romans 12:11—to never lag in zeal, but be aglow and on fire, serving the Lord enthusiastically.

I can remember reading *Tom Sawyer* in my English classes. Do you remember when Tom had to paint the fence? Tom didn't particularly want to whitewash the fence because he wanted to hang out with his friends. But he didn't get upset; he decided to con some of his friends into helping him. He went to painting that fence with so much enthusiasm that his friends wanted to do the same. Tom really had another plan—he was expecting them to jump in. Well, when his friends came around, he was whistling as though the job was something he was really enjoying. As his friends watched him, they all glared at each other as though to say, "Let's get into this." And so they did. Well, Tom's enthusiasm got him what he expected—he traded his paintbrush for a fishing pole.

I want to share the most astounding principle to living life fuller, living life by faith, even when you don't like your job. Simply put, face life enthusiastically—look for God to favor each and every day.

My life was miserable back in 2003, but one Sunday morning I was listening to Joel Olsteen, pastor of the Texas-based Lakewood Church. That particular morning he talked about "asking for God's favor." I had never heard of that concept. I began reading more about God's favor and I have been praying, believing, and walking in His favor ever since then. All praise to God.

Psalm 8:5 uses the word "honor." That word can be translated as "favor." If you look the word up in the dictionary it means to "assist, provide for, to assist in a special way," and "to receive special treatment." I was so excited to know that God, my Savior, the only person I have a covenant relationship with, wants to bless me with His favor. Wow! I was not about to throw that blessing or gift away. So, when I get up each morning, I seek God's favor over my day. For example, I might say "Lord, I am expecting your favor of goodness will follow me this day. I believe that your favor will cause me to radiate above others this day. I expect your favor will grant me peace today." Throughout my day, I speak His favor; and at the end of the day, I thank Him for His favor.

Another posture I take is that of visualizing how my day is going to be. Visualization is the process of creating vivid pictures in your mind. Visualization activates one's creative mind; it helps me create my day's activity. Using my vision I am able to see and reverse negative situations that are coming into my day. It's very simple. All I do is close my eyes and see myself accomplishing some specific goal. I understand that Jack Nicklaus, famed golfer, used visualization to help him win many of his golf tournaments.

I decided to find ways to fan the flame of my faith daily in the workplace and in my everyday walk. Enthusiasm and walking in the spirit of expecting favor from the Lord are the primary ways I fan the flame of my faith. These strategies have changed my attitude and countenance. I believe this is the reason God's favor and blessings have fallen on my table.

Wright

Rheba, where is your faith when going through the seasons of life?

Washington-Lindsey

David that is a loaded question that requires a lot of thought. Let me replay a typical week. My week may be filled with ups and downs, joy and sadness, disappointments and gladness, or laughter and tears. There are times when I simply want to fly away. The psalmist, David, speaks of flying away in Psalm 55:6: "And, I said, 'Oh that I had wings like a dove! For then would I fly away, and be at rest.'"

I would like to fly away and be at rest from the constant troubles that I hear about over the television—massive killings, suicides, wars, and more bloody battles, and more of the same. There are times when I don't want to hear any more. Yes, I pour out questions of "why" before the Lord, and He always reassures me that He is omnipotent, omnipresent, and omniscient; and that keeps my faith strong so that I am able to remain in a spirit of steadfastness.

Yes, there are plenty of times when the heaviness of the day's events saps my energy. I simply recall what Ecclesiastes 3:1–4a, 8a, says: "To everything there is a season and a time to every purpose under the heaven: A time to be born, and a time to die; a time to plant, and a time to pluck up that which is planted; a time to kill, and a time to heal; a time to break down, and a time to build up; a time to weep and a time to laugh . . . a time of war and a time of peace." So it is by faith that I—we—accept the seasons of living by faith. I am grateful that the seasons do not last forever; they only last for a season and they pass. When we weep during the seasons of trials, tribulations, sufferings, and war, we must realize that joy will come in the morning, because weeping only lasts for a while (from Psalm 30:5).

Wright

Rheba, you have established the fact that faith is an important ingredient for living an extraordinary life; it is the vein in your life, the substance you depend upon. I would like for you to expand upon what it means for you to live faith-minded.

Washington-Lindsey

I once read a quote by Josh Billings who wrote, "If there was no faith there would be no living in this world. We couldn't even eat hash with any safety."

Let me illustrate what it means to live faith-minded. God has already prepared to bless and help me in every area of my life. I've experienced so many devastating situations, and those situations have strengthened my faith in God. I've had no choice but to live faith-minded. I have found that when I've lived faith-minded I've seen God's blessings in all areas of my life: on my job, when I'm shopping; He gives me traveling mercies when I need a healing and in my relations with others.

As a specific example, David, I travel quite extensively and know the importance of being at the airport at least two hours in advance of my flight departure, but one particular trip to the airport was less than painless. My ticket to Africa was in my hand, my bags were packed, and I was leaving for the airport in plenty of time, enough time to sit and relax. That did not happen. I arrived at the airport, stood in line, and got to the check-in stand; the reservationist politely and calmly stated, "Dr. Lindsey, you are at the wrong terminal. You should be in the McCarran International Terminal. That terminal is about five minutes from here." She then proceeded to explain to my husband and me how to get to the international terminal. "The international terminal isn't close enough for you to walk. It is close but not that close. You are scheduled to board your flight in twenty minutes. There is not another flight after that one."

Then sudden fear and anger overwhelmed my spirit. I didn't think to pray. Disturbing thoughts of missing my flight quickly engaged my mind. Panic was rioting within me. As we moved swiftly through the airport to the parking garage, heading for the international terminal there was a long, brittle silence between us. When the international airport was in sight, our spirits were calm and we both confirmed God's favor of compassion was with us. We began to pray as we pulled my luggage from the car. Taking long purposeful strides, we ran through the airport to the ticket counter where we begged other passengers to let us pass. They did. God's favor was still with us. The ticket agent acknowledged that I was going to make the flight. The pilot was holding the plane for me. It seems that one of the companions begged the pilot to wait for me; she actually pleaded. God's favor was still working in my behalf.

When I live faith-minded I see God's miracles. Once when I was traveling along a dark, isolated stretch of a Texas highway, I experienced God's miracle and His favor of protection. A terrible thunderstorm had crossed East Texas and a hard freeze followed. I had never driven in such weather, so what lay ahead was not foreseen. The rain had turned the roads into sheets of black ice. As I drove across a bridge I failed to see the ice and crossed the bridge going at least seventy miles an hour. You can imagine what happened. Yep, you got it—my car skidded out of control and landed on a rail of the bridge. I carefully retrieved a flashlight, got out of the car, looked over the rail and discovered that there was a 100-foot drop to nowhere. In freezing cold weather, I began to cry out, "Thank you Lord for your protection."

My mother, who was traveling with me, said, "We could have been killed!"

When you experience a close call such as this one, it causes you to be thankful for life and for God's goodness. It was God who sent His angels to watch over His servant. I don't take His goodness for granted. When I'm living faith-minded, according to Psalm 23.6: God's blessings—His "goodness and mercy"—will follow me forever.

Being faith-minded has caused people to make exceptions to government policies. For example, several years back I traveled to China with a group of people. One of my purposes for taking the trip was to share my faith with those to whom God had pointed out the hope they could have in knowing Jesus Christ. So, with lots of prayer and fasting, I loaded up one of my suitcases with pocket-sized Bibles. David, if you know anything about international travel, you know that your luggage and documents are searched, especially when traveling in communist countries. At each checkpoint my roommate and another travel colleague would hold their breath that I wouldn't get caught. We must have passed three or four checkpoints as we journeyed into China; all of our bags were checked except the one with the Bibles in it. At each checkpoint the agent, who was armed with a gun, would motion for me to go through, and I went—carrying that one bag containing the Bibles. That's God's favor. I knew what would happen to me had I been caught, and I had made the decision to be willing to suffer the consequences if that had happened.

I ministered to people and offered them a Bible. With tears in their eyes, they accepted Christ and a Bible. I had faith to believe that the Lord's promise found in Psalm 34:22 was with me: "The Lord redeemeth the soul of his servants: and none of them that trust in Him shall be desolate" (KJV). I was carrying Luke 17:10 in my heart, that states, "So you also, when you have done everything you were told to do, should say, 'We are unworthy servants; we have only done our duty'" (NIV).

When you walk faith-minded you expect God's goodness to come your way. In fact, there are times when my confidence in God and my faith is so high that I let nothing get in my way. My faith is a testimony of the hope I have in the Lord. I keep my natural eye off my situation and keep my eyes on the Lord, giving Him praise and declaring His promises.

God blesses believers when they hope in His faithfulness, as Hebrews 10:35–36 sums up being faith-minded by confirming, "So do not throw away your confidence; it will be richly rewarded. You need to persevere so that when you have done the will of God, you will receive what he has promised" (NIV).

Wright

Is there one biblical character who has encouraged your faith?

Washington-Lindsey

Yes, there is. We all know the story of Joseph and the problem that came about because the gift of his "Technicolor" coat (see Genesis 37). Like Joseph, we all experience rejection and unfair or unjust treatment by others. When others hurt us we can choose to hold on to the pain and become bitter, take matters into our own hands, hold onto a grudge and promise to get even, or we can choose to trust God and allow His dominance to be established.

I've decided to watch God take care of those who have inflicted and who continue to inflict unfair treatment upon me. Sometimes I sit back and reminisce about the unfair treatment, whether it was from my supervisor because of race discrimination, rejection by my mother, or being unable to get a job promotion because of my principles. It all hurts. But I know that the Lord has promised to bless me for each injustice done to me. Wow, I'm going to be wealthy spiritually or however God chooses to bless me.

The story of Joseph inspires me because of his faith. Let's recap the highlights of his story. Joseph's life was filled with rejection and unfair treatment. He was thrown in jail on different occasions for crimes he did not commit. His brothers mistreated him because they were jealous of the beautiful, colored coat given to him by his father. His brothers sold him into slavery and then had the nerve to tell his father that a ferocious animal had killed him.

Can you imagine a brother or other family member mistreating you? Rejection by a family member is extremely difficult because family members are supposed to love one another, take care of one another, and be each other's primary support system.

Next, Joseph experienced rejection and unfair treatment from his employer. Remember how Joseph gained favor with Potiphar, the captain of Pharaoh's guard (Genesis 39:1a). Joseph was put in charge of all Potiphar's household and as a result, everything prospered. Unfortunately, Potiphar's wife liked Joseph too, but he continually ignored her advances. This made her angry so she falsely accused him of making sexual advances toward her. Potiphar believed her and had Joseph put into prison where he spent three years. Joseph was a remarkable interpreter of dreams, and his dreams came true. While in prison he interpreted dreams. It is important to know that prison can break one down, but in Joseph's case it bought him honor and respect. Joseph spent many years in prison and his faith in God remained strong.

Joseph was eventually released from prison and became second in command in Egypt. Because of his wisdom, he spared Egypt a great disaster by preparing for a famine. He became highly respected and powerful in the land. As you know, God continued to bless him for all the wrongs inflicted upon him. It had been years since Joseph had seen his family. Finally he was reunited with them, but he refused to take out revenge on them or reject them. Instead, Joseph told them, "But as for you, ye thought evil against me; but God meant it unto good, to bring to pass, as it is this day, to save much people alive"

(Genesis 50:20 KJV). You see, Joseph realized that his brothers thought they were harming him, but God took their jealous scheme and made it for good to accomplish His will, to save many lives. Joseph saw the wonderment and goodness of God that came forth out of being unfairly treated and rejected, and he believed in God's sovereign control.

After reading Joseph's story over and over, I came to realize that Joseph did not just skate through his rejection and unfair treatment without pain or suffering. Joseph wept as he went through his rejection and unfair treatment. He shed tears of sorrow, pain, and hurt. He wept when he saw his brothers, only this time his tears were tears of joy.

My Lord suffered unfair treatment and rejection. Most of those who held any place of prominence and authority rejected Jesus. "And he began to teach them [his disciples], that the Son of man must suffer many things, and be rejected of the elders, and of the chief priests, and scribes, and be killed, and after three days rise again." (Mark 8:31). Those who were respected and revered by the Jews rejected Him. I'm sometimes not much different than they were. Those who claimed to believe in Him rejected Jesus. Imagine what Jesus must have felt when Judas walked up to Him and used an act of love—the kiss—to betray him. The last words Judas heard from Jesus were these: "Judas, are you betraying the Son of Man with a kiss?" (from Luke 22:48).

David, I have felt the pain of those words, and I have been rejected and treated unfairly by someone who was a close friend.

Remember what the disciples did? They left Jesus. Each of them had committed to staying with Him, "Then all the disciples forsook Him, and fled," as reported in Matthew 26:56. Isn't that sad? Don't forget Peter. Three hours later He denied knowing Jesus, right in in His presence (see Luke 22:61). David, can you see the hurt in the eyes of Jesus? My heart still hurts because of the rejection inflicted upon Jesus, but it was all for the good.

As I look at the rejection of Jesus and Joseph it has been beneficial in a couple of ways: First, I am able to recognize that rejection comes with living on earth, especially as Christians. Second, I can rejoice in my rejection and unfair treatment instead of being sorrowful; as Jeremiah 31:13 says, "Then maidens will dance and be glad, young men and old as well. I will turn their mourning into gladness; I will give them comfort and joy instead of sorrow" (NIV).

Jesus understands my mourning and places my tears in a jar (Psalm 56:8). I know that He will heal my broken heart, and He has promised to never leave me or forsake me. I can count on Jesus.

Wright
How do you hold onto your faith when going through difficult times?

Washington-Lindsey
There's an old saying, "When the going gets tough, the tough get going." Quite the contrary with God's Word that tells us not to think of our difficulties or adversities as something that only happens to us, but we are to rejoice because of our difficulties. In our difficulties we are partakers of Christ's suffering. When His glory is revealed then gladness will overtake us (1 Peter 4:12–13).

When we think of difficulties in the human sense, it is difficult to rejoice. It took me a long time to internalize this Scripture. I thought that when I became a Christian there would be no difficulties in life—that my walk would be filled with joy and plenty of God's blessings. Then wham, the reality of being a Christian sank in. I have to admit that there were plenty of times I was discouraged, I felt down and just couldn't keep myself together. There was little smiling.

For example, in 2002 and 2003 I was going through some difficult times. My dreams were dashed to the ground, doors for job promotions were closing, opportunities to relocate began to slam shut, the flame in my marriage was growing dim, and my spiritual life needed rejuvenating. I refused to acquiesce, and believe that this was the way life was to be, like that old song, *"Que sera, será*—whatever will be will be, the future's not ours to see. *Que será será."*

But, God told me that He was preparing me for something bigger in my life. He went on to say, "Forget the former things; do not dwell on the past. See, I am doing a new thing! Now it springs up; do you not perceive it? I am making a way in the desert and streams in the wasteland" (Isaiah 43:18–19 NIV). When I heard that word I was immediately encouraged on the inside. My spirits stood as tall as a soldier, while on the outside I was bubbling over. I began to read God's Word more.

My prayer life changed and I began to spend more time on my knees, which meant waiting for God to speak to me. I returned to weekly fasting. Further, every day there was a smile on my face—I was dressed in the whole armor of God. I prayed, "Lord, you promised you would turn my situation around and work everything out for my advantage. You also said that all things work together for my good because I love you, Lord." I had to keep standing in faith. Ephesians 6:13–14 instructed me to stand—stand and pray. Now that's what I do. In fact, I begin every working day with Ephesians 6:11–17. I pray that Scripture and the Lord has blessed me with His favor in so many ways. I don't leave home without reciting that Scripture.

I think about David before he was given the throne and made King of Israel. He and his men were patrolling one day as God instructed them. While they were away, a band of robbers viciously destroyed their city by burning homes, looting, and bringing harm to women and children. The heart of David was broken he grieved out loud but decided he couldn't stay down. David knew that his faith was strong. According to 1 Samuel 30:6, David encouraged and strengthened himself in the Lord his God. In other words, David's faith prevailed in the midst of a difficult situation.

Then there are Paul and Silas when they were arrested, beaten, and tossed in jail. They didn't complain, yell, or hurl insults at the guards. They just began to sing hymns of praise to God. (See Acts 16:23–25.) In the midst of a difficult situation, their faith saw them through.

All of us are privy to God's power. We as His children have been blessed with favor that allows us to be conquerors, ." . . we are more than conquerors through Him that loved us" (Romans 8:37). However, a conqueror must be clothed with faith. God blesses believers when they stand strong in faith during difficulties. Psalm 62:5–6 gave me clear directions for what I need to do when going through difficult times: "My soul, wait thou only upon God; for my expectation is from Him. He only is my rock and my salvation: He is my defense; I shall not be moved" (KJV).

Wright
How does prayer affect your faith?

Washington-Lindsey
God's plan is for women to come to Him in prayer. God strongly encourages women to pray. David, I have learned the hard way that my battles are fought on my knees and that is how I have been victorious. There were many times when faced with problems I would run to friends, family, coworkers, my pastor, to complain. I would ultimately take their advice and then suffer the consequences later. In

Matthew 7:7–11, Jesus clearly emphasized the importance of prayer in the life of a Christian and Jesus instructed us to "ask, seek, and knock."

Unfortunately, I have missed so many opportunities and blessings because I failed to pray about all things, choosing to take the passive role in my prayer life. I would ask but would not seek through His Word or knock, which comes through prayer. I wasn't consistent either, meaning that if I went to Him in prayer it was once or twice because I knew what I wanted to do.

A prime example is I knew that I wanted to get married someday and I had my own idea of what type of man I wanted; but God knew what I needed. Anyway, I met a man and went to friends and family members to get their approval. Then I prayed about the matter. Well, by that time I was emotionally involved in the wedding planning and didn't have a listening ear for God. All during the planning time I knew God was trying to get my attention, but I continued planning. That's called ignoring the signs. I married and began to see what God was trying to show me a year later. To this day, I continue to see evidence of what He was trying to show me and I truly feel that I went against His will because I failed to pray over the matter.

I have learned that you cannot walk in faith without being in a constant state of prayer. I believe that because prayer is a form of communication between myself and the Lord, I want to talk to Him all through the day about whatever may be on my heart, believing by faith that He hears and will answer. I ask the Lord to search my heart and remove anything that is contrary to His will.

I realize now that sometimes He delays answering prayer requests even if my requests are within His will. That sounds strange, I know. If God sees something within me that is not right, such as a rebellious attitude, bitterness, unforgiveness, or any unhealthy habit, God puts my requests on hold until I am in a spiritual position to receive His blessing.

When we enter into prayer we must enter in a spirit of confidence making specific, not general requests. Remember the Sermon on the Mount as recorded in Matthew 5–7. Chapter 7, verses 7 through 8 specifically say: "Ask, and it will be given unto you; seek, and ye shall find; knock, and it will be opened to you: for everyone that asketh receives, and he that seeketh findeth; and to him who knocketh it shall be opened unto you" (KJV).

Prayer is not only asking but includes praising Him, adoring Him, and giving thanks to the Lord for what He has already done and will do. There is power in prayer. Prayer draws me closer to God, as it builds my relationship with Him. I am blessed as a result of being in persistent prayer or communication. I have made prayer an ongoing intimate relationship of conversation with the Lord. By building this intimate relationship, I am able to harness the Lord's strength when faced with Goliaths in my life. When I fight my battles on my knees, I win every time. Praise God from whom all blessings flow.

Wright

I remember reading several passages in the Bible where Jesus said, "Oh, ye of little faith . . ." What area of your life is the weakest in faith?

Washington-Lindsey

Well, accepting Jesus as Lord is the first step to faith. I must admit that I didn't have the kind of faith that can move mountains or the faith as a mustard seed. But as I grew as a Christian, my faith grew. Part of being a Christian is increasing in our faith.

Being a person of faith requires that we have a personal, intimate relationship with God. God desires for us to "know" Him. There were steps I had to take in order to grow in my faith and develop that intimate relationship that goes hand-in-hand with being a strong woman of faith. That meant I had to spend time with Him. I had to delight myself in Him (see Psalm 37:4 and Isaiah 58:14). My thought was, "I don't have that kind of time." But, there came a time in my life when I desired to grow my faith. I yielded to "delighting" in Him, trusting that He would draw near to me as He has promised in His Word (James 4:8) and that He delights in women who are seeking Him.

Psalm 63:1 says it so plainly, "O God, you are my God; early will I seek you; my soul thirsts for you; my flesh longs for you in a dry and thirsty land where there is no water" (NIV). God saw my earnestness and He began to draw me.

My lifestyle changed from walking as a woman of little faith who believed "God could," to a woman of great faith who believes "God will," and then ultimately to a woman who has obtained a more perfect faith that believes "God has done it."

I remember the story of Abraham and how God led him into a land of bountiful blessings because he had that more perfect faith. He will do the same for me as I trust Him and walk according to a "more perfect faith" (see James 2:22). It works.

Wright

Enduring faith means remembering God's love. How is your faith reflected in God's love?

Washington-Lindsey

"But let all who take refuge in you be glad; let them ever sing for joy. Spread your protection over them that those who love your name may rejoice in you" (Psalm 5:11 NIV).

When everything is on the up and up, meaning all things are going well, believing the Lord loves me is easy. However, when my trials come along leaving me frustrated, hurt, or angry, I have wondered where I stood with Him. In other words, where was His love for me? It was difficult for me to believe that a God whose Word is perfect and who has assured me of His love would cause harm or sorrow to come upon me. But, the first word of assurance states, "God is love" (1 John 4:8; 1 John 4:16) That means His love is consistent. While going through my longsuffering, I was challenged to believe that the Lord loves me.

Let me see if I can explain my thoughts on this. The mind is capable of entertaining voices, whether negative or positive. It was the negative voices that I had to watch out for. You see, David, the devil had a way of teasing me and he was causing me to undermine my trust in God by questioning God's love. His voice would ring out, "Well, if the Lord cared for you, He would never allow you to go through this heartbreak or sorrow."

As I look back at my pains I realize that they are characteristic of being a Christian, they represent who we are. When I became a Christian, I agreed to be subject to all kinds of misery, disappointments, troubles, oppositions, and temptations that troubled me and caused perpetual vicissitudes in my health and in my attitude. I had to realize that if I was going to grow my faith, *His love would need to be tough.* If I was going to be a member of His family, I would need to experience His love in a different form that was through longsuffering. I began to relate to what God went through while He walked on earth and what He went through while on the cross.

I know that I can depend on God's love because of His character—to love me is His nature. I find myself thinking of the cross when I dare to question the magnitude of His love for me.

Next, God's love is revealed through His Word and is a relevant part of His covenant expression. For example, Hebrews 13:5 states, "... for He Himself has said, 'I will never leave you nor forsake you.'" I had to remind myself that He knows what He is doing and why. Yes, there are times I may not understand His reason for allowing certain hardships, but I still know He is a loving God and all I have to do is trust Him.

Wright
Dr. Washington-Lindsey, I want to thank you for your time.

Washington-Lindsey
David, I have thoroughly enjoyed our conversation about remarkable women who walk in faith with God. I hope that something I have said will encourage, uplift, and inspire our readers to always walk in the spirit of faith no matter what life hands them.

About the Author

DR. RHEBA WASHINGTON-LINDSEY is a respected educator and author. She holds undergraduate degrees in sociology and psychology, master's degrees in education and communication studies, and a doctorate in intercultural studies. She has twenty-seven years of experience teaching grades five to twelve in addition to teaching at the college level in communication studies and multicultural studies. She developed and wrote an intercultural studies program, which received full accreditation, for teachers in Nevada. She has shared her wealth of experience with hundreds of teachers in the many professional development workshops she has taught.

Dr. Rheba (what she likes to be called), is a native of Texas, but grew up and has spent much of her adult life in Los Gatos, in the San Jose, California, area. She regularly attends church and has been a Sunday school teacher and youth advisor. She and her husband, Roy, whom she met in church, have been blessed with a wonderful daughter, Leah, who is married and lives in Germany. Rheba and Roy are the proud grandparents of two spunky grandsons.

Dr. Rheba is the author of two self-published books, *Teaching Culturally Diverse Children*, published in 2000; and *Teaching Isn't for Cowards*, published in 2007.

Dr. Rheba Washington-Lindsey is available for various speaking engagements—keynote addresses, professional staff development workshops, seminars or breakout sessions—and as a consultant.

Dr. Rheba Washington-Lindsey
E-mail: drlindsey@aol.com

Photograph by Roylens Photophaphy

Chapter 7

ANN JILLIAN

THE INTERVIEW

David E. Wright (Wright)
Today, we're talking with Ann Jillian, three-time Emmy nominee and Golden Globe Award-winning actress. In addition to being a motivational speaker, Ann is an accomplished performer in all areas of show business. She is a star of motion pictures, television, nightclubs, and the Broadway stage. She was voted one of the most admired women of the world in *Good Housekeeping Magazine*'s 1990 poll.

She is a volunteer performer for the St. Vincent Meals on Wheels program to feed the elderly, and she is a lifetime board member of the American Cancer Society and St. Jude Children's Hospital. Ann also works for the USO, the Disabled American Veterans Hospital visiting program, and many other charities.

In 1988, Ann won the Golden Globe Best Actress award for her starring role in the poignant NBC television biography, *The Ann Jillian Story*, which recounted her victory over breast cancer. Ann's motivational lectures are filled with humor, music, and information about life, health, and the joys of being a mom.

Ann Jillian, welcome to *Remarkable Women of Faith*.

Ann Jillian (Jillian)
Thank you so much for having me here.

Wright
Miss Jillian, most of our readers have seen you on television but may not be familiar with your background. Would you tell us how you started in the entertainment business?

Jillian
Actually, it has been more years ago than I care to remember. My mother, God love her, was an old-fashioned Lithuanian lady. When I was around four years old, we were living in Cambridge, Massachusetts, which is where I was born. My mother was watching me perform in a civic function that we had there in Cambridge. Some kids did some piano things, others did some poetic presentations, and I sang. When the music stopped, I didn't. I kept going. A man who was probably the size of Mickey Rooney, now that I think of it (although to me he was pretty big), came and took me off stage. My mother was in the wings, and she said, "Ah ha! We go to Hollywood!" So she uprooted the entire family and brought us to Hollywood.

I was discovered by coincidence. I know God had His hand in this plan somewhere. A letter came to the school that I was attending. It was from Art Linkletter's *House Party*. They gave it to the principal, who then chose a teacher, who then chose four children to be on the show. So I was on one of the original episodes of *Kids Say the Darndest Things*.

During that time, my mom met another mom who had an agent for her child. The woman suggested that we should do that, so my mom found an agent and I was on my way. I appeared in *Babes in Toyland, Gypsy*, and a number of other film projects.

I eventually went through a transitional period where I held back and stayed in school. Then I reemerged as an adult in Chicago in a project called *Goodnight Ladies,* where I did meet Mr. Mickey Rooney. He was about to start *Sugar Babies*, and he told the producers about me. I auditioned for them and I was given the superette lead. So my husband and I went to Broadway.

After our time on Broadway we came back to Los Angeles and started with *It's a Living* and the rest of those credits that you gave. I ended up with twenty-seven films under my belt and numerous specials. That's how it started out.

Wright

That's interesting. I'm going to go to the video store and check out the Natalie Wood version of *Gypsy* and try to find you.

Jillian

I played June. There are two versions of June, and I played the older one. There's also Louise—the part that Natalie played—who later becomes Gypsy. I was Natalie's sister.

Wright

In their early years, most successful people in any profession develop a strong sense of purpose and dedicate themselves to certain tasks or actions that will lead to specific results. What things did you do or what personal characteristics did you develop to ensure your success?

Jillian

It kind of unfolded, you know. It wasn't in my mind, as I recall. In fact, I was still searching. My mother had it her mind what I was going to do because she felt that what I had was a natural God-given talent. God was big in our house. She felt that it would be wrong not to develop those areas. Did I actually have an interest in them and think, "Oh, this is my goal"? No, I don't believe I did. I was just a good girl and I figured Mama *did* know best, and Dad worked toward that end.

It was probably somewhere around the time that I became an adolescent when I looked at my parents—I saw how hard they worked and I thought to myself, "What am I going to do? What are my strengths?" I kept hearing people say that in order to really have success, you must do what you love and what you do naturally. So I saw that my mother was actually quite right. I did, in fact, enjoy presenting a story in front of a camera and I did enjoy singing, so I thought, "All right, this is what I'm going to do."

I'm a relatively shy person, believe it or not, so I worked to counteract that shyness. I knew that it was not going to be a benefit to me if I were going into this business. This business, I knew, was something that would afford me the ability to take care of my parents later on in life and I wanted to do that because they are my family. Believe it or not, it was not a self-oriented thing. My goal was not to be a star; but my goal was to be a working actress who could help my family.

Wright
Did they live long enough to enjoy your successes?

Jillian
Yes, thank goodness. I have always prayed. Early on in my life, I remember going to a party after high school. One young man happened to be saying something about God answering prayers. I found myself listening to this individual, who said, "Oh come on. You don't believe that God really answers your prayers." Something—and I don't know where it came from—compelled me. I heard myself saying, "Sure, He does. He answers your prayers even if He says no." I realized at that moment how much I believed that God listens to us and God is there for us.

Everything I ever prayed for about my parents, He took care of. In their golden years I wanted them to not have to go through the pain of seeing their child debilitated by cancer. And the good Lord helped to restore me in that particular area.

I then became pregnant. It was almost like He gave me a stamp of approval after fifteen years of childless marriage. So seven years after my breast cancer, I had a child—my one and only son. And then I prayed, "Please, God, let my parents be able to know him, that he would be old enough to remember them. And He did." So all the way down the line, it was really other-oriented. I knew that this was what He gave me to work with and that this was what I must go after. So I continued. That was my goal—to take care of my family.

Everything I did, I did basically because I knew that I had to. If I was shy, if I was scared, if I was nervous about going out on stage, I would say a prayer ahead of time. I would offer it up to Him, and then I would say to myself, "You have to do this, because there is no other way that you will be able to take care of them the way you want to." So I went out there and I did it. Each job was a step to the next, and I literally learned on the job.

Wright
How did your relationship with God affect your career choices along the way?

Jillian
It was a very conscious choice that I made—when I was able to be in that position to make choices—to choose projects that had hopeful

endings or that had hopeful feelings throughout. A lot of them were true stories.

Wright

Neither my wife nor I will admit to it, but we are hooked on a television show called *Inside the Actors Studio*.

Jillian

Yes.

Wright

And that is the recurring theme with all the famous actors who are on that show. At first you have to do anything and everything anybody asks you, but then you get your own choice of scripts. That must be wonderful when you get to that point.

Jillian

It's funny, because everybody is at his or her own level. I won't get, and didn't get (much to my dismay) the scripts that perhaps Meryl Streep or Sally Field or any number of other actresses at that time got. But in my area, what I did get was abundant enough. And I figured if they were coming to me, God wanted me to make choices, and I did make the choices. I hope that they were in accordance with what He wanted me to do. I also had a few scripts (more than a few) that came to my door and I said, "Absolutely not. Why would you think that I would do that?"

Wright

When I talked to Jennifer O'Neill last month, I found that her Christian beliefs cost her a lot in her career, especially the Hollywood part of it. She was on *The View* some time ago, I think. She took a stand against abortion. The other four or five ladies on the show said that they were really angry and that Jennifer could never appear on *The View* again.

Jillian

What?

Wright

But the network started getting phone calls saying that Jennifer O'Neill was great and that they agreed with her, so they asked her back. *The View* asked her back after saying she would never appear there again. So she's taken some heat for her Christian beliefs.

Jillian

Well, God love her! And I know that He does, because she's out there upholding His will. I'll tell you what, we are all one day going to meet our Maker, and we all will be held responsible for His will. That's the way I feel, obviously, so there you go.

Wright

Good Housekeeping Magazine named you as one of the most admired women in the world. Of course, to me and others, that's really impressive, especially when you consider other women who hold that distinction. As a shy person, how did that make you feel?

Jillian

I was very honored, because if you take a look at that year and the women with whom I shared that honor, I did not see myself in the league of someone like a Mother Teresa. There were other women who were in serious areas of politics and so forth. These were women who were quite accomplished. So for me to be put in the same league was a tremendous honor. I believe that others saw admirable things in what I was doing.

I would imagine that it was probably because of the way I handled my breast cancer. It was probably more about how I continued a mission to remind women of the importance of early detection and swift medical action. I think that those two things probably elevated how people perceived me in that respect; but I was and am still quite honored—very honored—and I will always remain quite surprised that I was voted in that way.

Wright

I watched my wife go through a struggle with colorectal cancer for two years, and she finally made it through. Everyone, including me, thought she would not. We hoped that she would and prayed that she would, but there were a few times when I doubted. So trust me, you really *do* deserve the honor.

Jillian

The honor is shared because everybody who has to go through that kind of a challenge—a cancer challenge or any kind of a life-threatening or a life-altering illness—has to come up to the plate. They have to live through this, so anything that I endured is only representative of all those silent heroes nobody knows about because they don't make their living in front of a camera. I happened to, and perhaps that is what placed me in that position; but I share that with your wife. I share it with all the people—all the ladies, our daughters, our aunts, our sisters, our wives, and the wives throughout the world—who have ever had to go through that.

Wright

Will you tell us about your struggle with cancer and how it immediately affected your life?

Jillian

Cancer is a family thing. It is a struggle that everybody in their own way has to go through once it hits one person in the family.

I was raised in a very religious family—a faith-filled family. When I developed cancer, it validated my beliefs. The things I learned through catechism and through my early years I had to pull up and out of me and use as my anchor. And the cancer actually validated everything that I was taught to believe—the idea that every single second of life is worth living; the idea that life is sacred from the very beginning to the very end; that our good Lord is really in charge; that many things I believed became validated by that experience.

An interesting thing occurred. I was a compassionate person beforehand, both intellectually and in my heart, but when I developed cancer and walked through the fears, walked through the challenges, walked through the treatments and the sufferings that I endured, my compassion became an extremely deep one. All of a sudden, I was united with the sufferings of all of humanity.

I had people who sent me letters from around the world, telling me about their own experiences. And I literally had to take time off from the hours that I spent reading at home after the surgery because it took my breath away. I so deeply felt their struggles and their sufferings, and it really takes what you have on the surface to a very deep level.

I feel that there was growth in it. You know, there were many dark days that my family and I had to endure and, obviously, cancer is not a good thing—anything that is life-threatening like that is not a good thing. But like the mythological phoenix rising from the ashes, something does become resurrected in a time like that. It is this spirit—the human spirit—and it facilitates the ability to grow. Those kinds of challenges facilitate the ability to grow, and that is *always* a good thing.

Wright

My wife and I were in a meeting a while ago with several people at church. We were discussing hardships and things that people had gone through. My wife made the statement, as you just said, that even though cancer is horrible and even though the pain and all the suffering is terrible, she would not give anything for having gone through the experience. And I almost thought she was nuts, but as I looked at her, I could tell she was dead serious.

Jillian

I understand her. It is not something that you would wish on anyone or yourself, but in the throes of it, you can only look upon it to see what redemptive value it has. There is inherent in all of our struggles a redemptive value, and obviously God, who is in all parts of our lives, every day of our lives, wanted us to glean from it what we could.

My suffering was, all of a sudden, united with the suffering of everybody—of all of mankind—in various different ways because I felt close to that suffering.

It also became very clear that I could not sit and complain about it because my suffering was elevated to Christ's suffering. That made my suffering sacred because at that moment on the cross He elevated all of mankind's suffering. Up until that time, we didn't know why we suffered. In our minds, in our hearts, we thought, "How on earth could this suffering possibly mean something good?" And yet, out of that horrific death on that cross, He made it a source of salvation for all of us. So I looked at that. I thought to myself, "There's nothing that I can suffer here that can be more than what He suffered there." So that helped me get through it.

Wright

My wife and my family were absolutely overwhelmed and overcome by all of the prayers and acts of kindness that were directed toward us during those times. I couldn't help but say that it was, in some way, modeling what Christ did to have that much kindness. I have never asked anybody for anything, but boy, I tell you what, people just started helping and doing things and calling and writing. And people were praying around the world. There were stories of churches of 5,000 and 6,000 people getting together in Guatemala and other places and praying for her. It was unbelievable. Did you experience that sort of thing?

Jillian

Yes! Yes! It was an amazing, amazing phenomenon. Within the first week, we had 60,000 letters. Over the course of time, I'm sure it went up to somewhere around 300,000 letters. But I got the prayers. I had people from Israel sending me prayers, and they had cedar trees planted in my name. And you know, that this is a godly thing. I wept. I spent a lot of time weeping because I was so totally stunned and so totally touched by what came through. You're right, it's a magnificent thing to see how the spirit of so many people will come up and help—the spirit of people reaches out to help others.

Wright

How much of your recovery do you think was an act of faith?

Jillian

To me, *everything* is connected, so I have to say 100 percent. I keep coming back to faith because to me, He is the source of all good. So whatever recovery came to me came through the hands, minds, and instruments of those people through whom He works.

We are His instruments if we are open to it. It's like ripples. Somebody throws a pebble in a still lake, and you see the ripples going out. Some people are out in the community, and they are compelled by their inner selves to do something for the community. Some are more vocal; some work just through writing. It doesn't matter how, but we all ripple out into our extended families—into our communities, the nation, the world. It comes through an inspiration, I believe, and that inspiration to me is God. He works through His people—our doctors, our nurses, our researchers, and everybody. They are touched by God. They are kissed by God, and they are commissioned by that kiss to go out and fulfill a mission that only they can fulfill.

Some of us are listening; some of us are not. Some of us may hear well early on in life, and some may find it by stumbling and perhaps by talking with others. But we cannot stop talking. We cannot stop writing. We cannot stop living in the example that He wants us to live.

But to get back to the point, let me say I believe that faith is the anchor. Faith is what everything is built upon. If I could give anything to my son, it would be the gift of introducing him to a strong faith and then weaving it into each and every single part of his daily life. I am a Christian. I am Roman Catholic. To me, it's not just something that I do every Sunday when I go to mass. My faith has become a part of my very identity. My birth name is Ann Jura Nauseda. Ann Murcia is my married name, and Ann Jillian is my professional name, but whatever name I have, I am this woman of faith who is a part of every fiber of my being.

My Catholicism is a part of me and my very identity. I cannot extricate myself from that. It's who I am, and having that strength gives me strength of purpose. It lights how I see things in life, and it helps to light the decisions that I am going to make in life. The one thing that we have (and I can be very happy in talking about it as far as the Christian faith is concerned) is that when we are knocked down to our knees, we are able to get up again. We do get knocked down on our knees—nobody is perfect. The only One who was perfect died on the cross on that Good Friday. But we are able once again, with that faith, to breathe in, think of our Lord, and move on ahead. That is the gift I wanted to give to my son.

Is faith a part of everything in my life? It is the moving factor in my life. I've said very often that life is a tenderizing process and a series of lessons in humility; so perhaps when we come back again to our most vulnerable selves in our old age, we will actually come to know the truth of that saying that there is strength in weakness. And faith leads you there. Faith takes you beyond. That's what it means to me.

Wright
When I consider the help we get from each other, the information we get from each other, and the confidence we receive from each other, I'm reminded of one of your friends, Bob Hope. I read a beautiful story you wrote about Mr. Hope that I would like for you to share with our readers. Would you do that?

Jillian
Oh, I would love to share it. It'll be paraphrased from the actual writing, of course, because I don't remember the exact words. The

story I will relate took place in 1983. As a child I had always felt that one was never really officially a part of this thing called "show business" until one was asked by Bob Hope and the USO to perform for our peacekeeping troops or our troops who were actually in action. My turn came in 1983, when the hot spot was just off the shores of Beirut, Lebanon. I was asked to come and perform with the USO and Bob for the Sixth Fleet during Christmastime and visit each and every one of the ships with him.

So there he was. It was one of the evenings when we were going back to what we affectionately referred to as the "Beirut Hilton," which was actually the USS Guam anchored off shore. We had just done a performance on one of the other ships, and the director decided he wanted to get a sunset shot that evening, with me singing *Silent Night* with the sunset behind me and the rest of us there. But since it was now curfew, we had to go back on a Foxfire boat instead of a plane. There were boxes of ammunition there. Bob sat down, and all of us were "shaking in our boots," because we had no idea what was about to come up. It was dark. We were on an unfamiliar ocean. I understand there were some pretty nasty things in that ocean. The Navy Seals were saying, "If we capsize, do not call out. We'll find you." And even the idea that these wonderful men would save us didn't help me much.

But then I looked at Bob when we started to go into the ocean, and the wake of the ocean was behind him. There was this eerie kind of a red, low-cast light that was illuminating him, and he was sleeping. Our "old man of the sea" was sleeping and taking it all in stride. I thought to myself, "I am so lucky and so privileged to be here with him." Because I knew that he was charmed, I was going to stay with him. In the sheer darkness, and while our armies were shaking, he was deeply and rhythmically breathing and sleeping and taking all of those naps that he took so well.

He woke up when we started to slow down, and out of nowhere, this immense structure—a very surrealistic sight, the side of this metal monster, the USS Guam—was lit up. The guys got out and docked the Foxfire boat to a platform dock. We were supposed to jump onto that. Well, I took a look at Bob and thought, "You've got to be kidding! If you jump onto that platform and you miss the timing, you're going to get smashed!"

Bob was having his feet massaged to get him going. He got up and he was our fearless leader. He went forward and without missing a beat, he jumped. He was in his eighties at the time. So I looked at my husband, and we were duly embarrassed and ashamed of what we had been thinking, so we took the jump.

The next thing we saw was a rope and metal ladder that fell down several stories along the side of ship, and I said, "No! You've got to be kidding me! We're going to go up this?" So they attached it, and sure enough, Bob started going up. Our pied piper started going up there. One guy said, "Just don't look down." Well, my palms were sweating (I hate going up ladders). Of course, the first thing you do after someone gives you an instruction is do exactly what they just told you *not* to do. I looked down, and I found out why I'd been told to not look down. I immediately froze to the ladder. I looked up and I saw Bob going up very calmly and over onto the deck of the ship. I thought, "Okay, I can't stop here. I've got to keep going." So I kept looking up, and I thought, "If he can do it, I can do it. If he can do it, I can do it." I got up there, and I got onto the USS Guam.

I remember when we were performing on stage there. At one time in our history, I remember there was a controversy as to whether or not this was a publicity thing that Bob did for himself or something that he had his heart in. I must tell you without a doubt that his heart was in it. Oh, I saw it many times. I would be in the wings, watching him.

I remember one time specifically. Bob must have felt that somebody's eyes were on him. There he was, in the light, watching the people watching Vic Damone singing, and then he sensed it. He turned and he caught me looking at him. He smiled, and his eyes were full of tears. He said with such love and such devotion, "They're my guys and gals." I could see there were volumes spoken in what he told me. What his face told me was that he considered it a privilege to be there to perform for them. He considered it a privilege to bring laughter to our sons and daughters and sisters and brothers and fathers and mothers who had come upon humorless times, at a time when a little bit of home was the one thing that they wanted for Christmas.

Wright
Right!

Jillian
He brought it there to them and had been doing so for many years, long before I came on the scene. That was the last time he officially went out—that trip during Operation Desert Shield. That was the

last time, and I was privileged enough to witness that. So Bob gave a lot of people a lot of memories. He knew what his position would do for them, but he also introduced them into an area of life that he felt the privilege of feeling.

He introduced all of us to the things that satisfied him on the inside, and he said, "See here. This is what it's all about. This is what is reaching out to those who want a sense of family right now." He was a great patriot, as we all know. He came from England to this country, and his adopted country gave him a beautiful, beautiful future.

Our country is the most wonderful, fabulous country, filled with wonderful, fabulous people, especially those who are willing to go out and uphold the precepts of our country and fight for it and fight for what we believe in—freedom. He wanted to give back to that because he knew what this country meant to him and what this country gave to him and made possible for him.

Wright
It was a great tribute.

Jillian
You know, I think that he's up there in the arms of our Savior, who is saying, "Well done, my good and faithful servant." It was a privilege to be with him, and I thank him for giving us the memories, and for inviting my family to the shows. My mother and father were invited up to Bob's home in Palm Desert. My father was introduced to the Blue Angels and took pictures with them, so it was a thrill for him and my mother to see all this.

My son now has the ability to take a look at the memories I have. Bob's wife, Dolores, always loved the picture of me on the cover of one of the magazines—I think it was *Good Housekeeping* or maybe it was *Ladies Home Journal*. But anyway, I was holding Andy when he was just an infant. Dolores asked to put it up with her collection of the Madonnas in her home. I was so thrilled about that. You know, I have a frame that was inscribed by them for my son, so he will also have something to talk about with his children.

Bob left a legacy for a lot of people, and he will be grievously missed. I loved him and Dolores dearly.

Wright
I know that you are changing peoples' lives as you go about the country presenting your topics: "I Never Had a Bad Day in My Life,"

"Surviving and Thriving," and "The Winner in You." I know how rewarding that must be, but has talking to and helping people changed you in any way?

Jillian

Talking to other people, I believe, is always a good thing. When I go out, I may talk, but I also have a question-and-answer period. That question-and-answer period runs the gamut. I mean, they ask me about being a mother. They ask me about my medical history. I also get people who come up and tell their stories. They tell of their struggles and their triumphs. When we go out there and talk, my energy is totally drained out of me; but I get reenergized by the inspiration I get from the stories of others. So I think it's a cycle. I think it's a circle of breathing out and breathing in—breathing out the information and hopefully, the inspiration and entertainment, and then breathing in the reenergizing and refueling from other people. It's other-oriented, and that's always energizing.

Wright

What a great conversation on faith. We've been talking today with actress, entertainer, and speaker Ann Jillian. Ann, I really appreciate the time you've taken with me today. I know how busy you must be. This has really been enlightening for me, and I am sure it will be for our readers as well. Thank you so much for being with us today.

Jillian

It's been a pleasure talking with you, David. Thank you very much.

About The Author

ANN JILLIAN is a three-time Emmy and Golden Globe Award winning actress and singer. Since 1985, she has added motivational speaker to her impressive list of credits, addressing business, medical, professional, and women's groups with her own unique blend of humor and inspiration. Ann's programs are fun, informative, and flexible to the clients' needs.

Good Housekeeping Magazine named her one of the most admired women of the world. Her prowess extends from the world's concert halls, to feature film and the Broadway stage. She has starred in over twenty-five television movies, and made hundreds of other television appearances. Her television movie, *The Ann Jillian Story,* which recounted her victory over breast cancer, was the number one film of the television season. More importantly, it delivered Ann's message about the hopeful side of breast cancer to its millions of viewers. With the birth of her son after cancer, she now adds the title "Working Mom" to her impressive accomplishments. In addition, she is the President of her own production company, 9-J.

Ann Jillian
Andy Murcia, Manager
Phone: 818.501.0807
Fax: 818.501.1887
P.O. Box 57739
Sherman Oaks, CA 91413
www.annjillian.com

Chapter 8

Reverend Diannia Baty
"Lady Diannia"

THE INTERVIEW

David Wright (Wright)
Today we are talking with Reverend Diannia Baty. "Lady Diannia," as she is known by her students and followers, is an intense "in-your-face" teacher of the divine connection. Her students and followers love her style of delivery. She has dedicated her life to the study of theology and spirituality and started on a mission to teach others about what and who they really are. In the course of her studies of many mentors and master teachers she experienced Oneness within her soul and has been transformed. She now only wishes to be of service to others.

Everywhere she speaks, peoples' lives are transformed as she teaches them the tools and practices to be in a higher state of consciousness and in vibrational alignment with the Creator. These tools and practices are designed to evolve your soul, your mind, and your life. Lady Diannia's devoted students declare publicly that their lives are not the same, that they look at life differently, and have a stronger connection to God. They say that they finally "get it" and they have peace and joy in their lives consistently for the first time. Those who attend her workshops and speaking engagements say they could listen to her speak all day. She has transformed lives with her words.

Lady Diannia, welcome to *Remarkable Women of Faith*.

Diannia Baty (Baty)

Thank you, David. I am so grateful for this opportunity.

Wright

How did you get started in teaching spirituality?

Baty

Well, it was a convoluted path at best. I guess since I was about five years old I have had the ability to see and hear what you would call "spirit entities." I would have visions and know things that no five-year-old should know. Whenever I mentioned these things to my mother, she would validate my experience but tell me to keep it quiet. My mother had psychic ability so she knew the pitfalls involved with this gift.

What most people don't understand is that all of us—each and every one of us—has this gift. If you choose to deny it, then go ahead; but you can't deny the facts. There are very few mothers who haven't experienced a feeling that something was wrong with their child and it turned out to be right. You may suddenly experience a feeling of dread for no obvious reason and it won't go away and then later get a call that someone you love has passed on. The phone may ring with a call from someone you were thinking about and have not heard from in a long while. You may also find yourself walking toward the phone to answer it only to have it ring after you reach to pick it up.

My mother told me that people would not understand, so after a period of time I tried to ignore it or deny it. If you have this ability you cannot make it go away. I learned to live with it, and I kept it quiet for the major part of my childhood.

As I grew older I was exposed to many religious teachings. My parents were religion shoppers. My father followed the construction trade and we traveled around quite a bit, so wherever we landed our parents would send us to the nearest church. I was exposed to Baptist, Lutheran, and Pentecostal churches just to name a few. My parents didn't go to church with us very much but they sent us. My parents had five children and that gave them the opportunity to have some time alone. They used the church as a babysitter.

All these religious teachings were confusing at best; but always in the background was this psychic and intuitive ability that had manifested itself in my life at such a tender young age. I remember being told in church one day that anyone who had this gift was evil and should be avoided.

I remember questioning a Sunday school teacher about why such a powerful force like God would need arms and legs like we have and was she sure that God was a man? She chastised and embarrassed me in front of all the other children and told me that I was a bad girl for asking such questions and to never do it again. She told me that I had insulted God and had committed a horrible sin.

I started questioning what I was being taught because no one—the pastors of the churches, the Sunday school teachers, or even my mom and dad—could get his or her facts straight about God, Jesus, Heaven, or Hell. Everyone seemed to be contradicting each other and themselves. I was being taught that God was separate from me and that I needed a middleman to get through to this power and this energy. I never felt that I would be good enough or holy enough to ever be with God.

I always felt inadequate. When I got older the psychic ability got extremely strong. I was fortunate enough to meet some incredible spiritual teachers. They taught me the true meaning of spirituality, psychic ability, freewill, and how all this fits into the Divine Creator's plan. They showed me a very clear path to God. They helped me to understand what my abilities were. They showed me that the abilities were a gift from God and they were to be used in service to mankind.

Wright

You have had a lot of trauma in your life. Would you say these experiences have been instrumental in where you are today and if so, how?

Baty

Absolutely. I was the oldest of five children in an extremely dysfunctional family. My father was an alcoholic. My mother was very codependent. She had her own traumatic secrets that she kept to herself until she was almost sixty years old.

Being the oldest I was given a lot of responsibilities. My mother was sick often. I became the little mother to all my siblings and was never really allowed to be a child. I was always being told "keep the other children quiet, your dad is hung over," "help me cook," "make the beds," "change your baby brother's diaper," "wash the dishes," and a whole cornucopia of chores with a tremendous amount of responsibility. There is a photo of me at about five years old with an apron tied under my armpits, standing on a chair washing dishes.

My father was a tyrant and his anger terrified all of us. I could not wait for the day I could leave home. So I did what most young people do in a situation like that—I took my first opportunity to get out. I married the first man who asked me (just before my seventeenth birthday) with my parents' permission. I walked right out of the frying pan into the fire. I ended up being widowed before I was twenty-one years old and had buried two children. I stared death right in the face and then throughout the years, I had a lot of bad relationships.

I lived an unconscious life and I had a lot of trauma that included deception, verbal abuse, bankruptcy, being cheated on, being lied to, and being used. Later in life I was widowed again when my husband of ten months committed suicide with a shotgun in our home. I came home from work and found his body. I will spare you the graphic details.

You would think one would buckle under these kinds of experiences, but they made me very strong and they made me value life. My experiences made me see that you can rise above all negative circumstances. When I teach, counsel, and coach people, I tell them that I know how they feel, and I do. Those are not just words—I really can empathize with them; I have been there.

You must make a choice and it is simple—do you want to be a survivor or a victim? As a reverend and a spiritual teacher, who better to help others than someone who has really been there?

Wright

You teach spiritual development classes. Would you tell us more about this?

Baty

Throughout my life people have come to me with their problems and life issues. When I started in earnest down the path of spirituality, I started sharing what I had learned. I was asked by quite a number of people to start teaching. Soon I started some teaching in my home. The group grew and grew. Everyone was telling me that they were experiencing such peace and joy with what they were learning. What I was teaching them empowered their lives. I became ordained as a reverend as a natural consequence of that.

I am not a soft-spoken speaker. I want you to "get it." I am very observant and in the past I noticed that almost as soon as people drove off the church parking lot the negativity started. You could say that what I teach is how to live your life after you leave the parking lot. I give you some real meat and potato spiritual development tools that work in daily life, in the workplace, or in your personal relationships.

It appears that most people live their lives by default but we are not computers. We use our minds with a default setting, however. Many people are still being affected by childhood upbringing. They can't seem to leave the past behind and indeed don't have a clue how to forgive and why. The churches teach we must forgive but don't tell us how and why. We are taught many things but the real nitty-gritty is how. I teach people to be in a high state of gratitude every day from the moment they awake until they go to sleep. It is very difficult to be in the lower mental states of anger, worry, depression, etc. if you are busy being grateful.

I also stress meditation. Meditation is extremely important in spiritual development. It is a sure-fire, proven way to be in profound contact with God. It is also the way to know yourself. I also consider it to be an intense, sincere form of prayer. It is time to use your mind in the proper way and to stop letting your mind use you. Take control and also take full responsibility for your life and how you create it. Here is an eye-opener: you *do* have a choice!

Wright

How do you define spirituality?

Baty

Spirituality is a very personal, concentrated effort to be in contact with your Creator on a daily basis.

Wright

How do you remain so peaceful and calm?

Baty

Well, the number one way is that I walk the walk and talk the talk—I practice what I teach. I do meditation a lot and I also do guided mediation in my classes because some people need a facilitator to learn how to do this. I produce CDs with guided mediation as well.

When you start practicing mediation and go within, that is how you get to know yourself. That is how you really get in contact with your Creator. It is within, not out there or "up there." When you quiet the mind and go within it is the most powerful tool you can use to be at peace. After a period of time, your whole life becomes mediation and a prayer. It is the only way to truly live your life.

I also practice gratitude and non-judgment. The gift of life and using my free will to be of service makes me very joyful.

Wright

If there was only one thing you would say to anyone to make an impact spiritually, what would it be?

Baty

That if you want your life to change, you must make the effort to do so. It does not happen automatically. One must say, "I've had enough of living my life that way. I've had enough of the pain, I've had enough of the trauma, and I've had enough of whatever it is that was making me unhappy."

If people are truly at the point where they cannot take it anymore and they do not understand, they must make the effort to understand. They must go to spiritual teachers and read the books and listen to the tapes and find out for themselves what is going on in the world and in their minds and hearts.

There is a spiritual evolution taking place in the world right now. It is all about learning what and who we are. We are brought into being to create wonderful lives. We are physical, emotional, and spiritual manifestations of God. We must start to honor that. It is time to stop blaming everyone and everything else for all our problems. It is time to find a way to be of service to our fellow human beings. There are so many ways to open our spiritual aperture.

Wright

You say that you have a very personal and intense relationship with your Creator. Will you try and describe it?

Baty

It is just an amazing thing to try to describe, but hopefully I can bring about a sense of excitement for someone to see the possibilities of how it can be.

As I move through my days in contact with my Creator, I am being sent knowledge constantly through my heart. I am being sent messages of affirmation and gifts of joy. I am having guidance channeled through me in the books, meditations, articles, and the poetry that I write. I also channel this divine energy when I paint. I have the presence with me all the time. It is just very powerful. My life becomes a prayer. I feel this peace and power and joy with me all the time. I speak to my Creator as I speak to you. It has transformed my life as I shifted from belief to knowing that I am a part of this force. I am not just a physical body. What I am is a soul. When you shift into a "knowing" like that, your life is never the same.

I have become hyper-aware of my surroundings. All my senses have become greater than before. I have become what some would call "enlightened."

Wright

You are a very creative person and have written many articles and produced some CDs as well. Are you planning anything else in the future?

Baty

Yes. I have written a children's book called the *King with Thousands of Shoes*. This is a book for the eight- to fourteen-year-old range; but ironically, many adults I have shared it with just love it.

I never know what I am going to write. I cannot take credit for everything that I create. For the book mentioned above, I went to my keyboard and I wrote the title and stared at the blank screen; but within the space of three hours, there were sixty-four rhymed verses of this story. Now, it is not easy to rhyme anything when you deliberately set down to do it, but this one just flowed like a river.

The story is for children and is about materialism. So many children are into materialism and that is not what makes one happy. This story is to drive home that point.

I have an illustrator actually working with it, but I have not found a publisher yet, however, I am working on that. I asked my Creator to manifest it for me and that will be coming.

I am also working on a spiritual awareness book, called *An Unconscious Life*. It is all about what I teach.

The third book in process is a cookbook called *Cooking for the Angels*. I am still working on this one. When it is in hardcopy, it will be sold to support the ministry (I am a consecrated bishop with New Life Path Ministries).

New Life Path Ministries teaches from a tenet of love and service. The ministry has a spiritual retreat in a huge 1920s home with a garden grotto in Granite Quarry, North Carolina. We accommodate only three people at a time. We have a nominal charge daily. We serve breakfast and provide prayer, healing work, and coaching for life and spiritual issues. My associate, Reverend Ariadne Romano, and I are collaborating on some new CDs of guided meditations for specific issues such as weight loss, pregnancy, aging, and stress among others.

Wright

How would you describe a typical day in your life using your spiritual practices?

Baty

Well, my life is anything but typical by generic terms. I start my day before I put my feet on the floor. I start in a state of gratitude. I lie there and start voicing what I am grateful for. Then I put my feet on the floor. I want to start my day in the right vibration. I want to say very quickly here that when you start with gratitude, it feeds upon itself and it keeps you in a joyful state. If, for example, you have a flat tire, be in a state of gratitude for the car rather than cursing the flat tire. That is how I start my day.

It has been said that we think approximately 60,000 thoughts a day. That is way too much mind chatter. No wonder there is so much anxiety and depression in our society. Imagine how glorious life would be if you took control over the nature and the quality of your thoughts.

I write what I call my "spirit letters" and I sit down with my journal and write my general thoughts. I ask if there is anything that the Holy Spirit wants to share with me. I wait and then I write what I have been given.

I walk out to my back door and look at my bird feeders and I am constantly in awe of all the things that have been given to me. I stay in a state of joy throughout my entire day. This keeps me in a high spiritual vibration and creativity just flows. I have a lot of "God Jobs" to do.

Wright

What is your biggest fear?

Baty

That is a simple one: that I will not have enough time left to do all the things that I desire to do—to create all the things that I want to help humanity.

I am very blessed right now. At this point in my life I am associated with New Life Path Ministries. I just recently became involved to help establish this ministry in North Carolina. The woman who was instrumental in establishing this ministry is now living in my home. We are offering services, classes, workshops, and retreats here. We want to help people to rise above the unconscious illusions of living and help guide them to awareness and joy.

Wright

Reverend Diannia, is there anything else at all that you would like to share with people that may help them along with their spiritual development? Also, would you tell us what your favorite quotes are?

Baty

I would like to say that life is such a profound gift. You were never meant to suffer. You can create a heaven here on earth right now. You don't have to wait for it. You have the power to create. It is your spiritual birthright. Shift to the power within your "higher self." This is the self that is connected to the essence of God. You are a divine creation. Learn, question, and read all you can to discover what and who you are. You are not your job or your possessions. You are pure energy. You are a soul. You are not the past—you are the now. Learn how to get into alignment with God's energy. Wrap your mind around the fact that the universe is infinite. There is no end to it. There are galaxies and stars beyond counting. The power that created this created you and gave you free will! How are you using your gifts?

My two favorite quotes are as follows: "knowledge is power." The second is: "The journey of a thousand miles starts with a single step." It is time you start your journey.

Wright

What a great conversation. I appreciate your time and wish you well.

About the Author

REVEREND DIANNIA BATY is a lifetime member of International Speakers Association and a consecrated Bishop of New Life Path Ministries. Reverend Baty is an accomplished artist and is a member of the Caroline York World of Art. Her artwork is sold and represented by Caroline York-Adams. Reverend Diannia Baty recently became affiliated with Lisa Thomas, founder and president of The Power, Passion, and Purpose Group and is a member of the P3 Connection, a non-profit organization dedicated to "Every woman living a life of Power, Passion, and Dreams Come True." The P3 Connection is a network of diverse, yet like-minded women who collaborate in a safe environment to further their areas of interest, passion, and vision.

She resides In Granite Quarry, North Carolina, and is available for spiritual readings and coaching sessions via the phone, Internet, or in person.

Reverend Diannia Baty
New Life Path Ministries
P. O. Box 231
Granite Quarry, NC 28072
Phone: 704.209.6430
E-mail: ladydiannia@alltel.net
www.divine-spirit.net
www.newlifepathministries.org
www.carolineyork.com
www.thep3group.com

Chapter 9

Desiree Carter

THE INTERVIEW

David Wright (Wright)
Today we are talking with Desiree Carter. Desiree is a pastor, author, keynote speaker, and workshop facilitator. She is an image consultant, known as a "life force mechanic."

Desiree spends the bulk of her time helping others sift through old tapes in an effort to unveil old paradigms that keep them from being successful in both business and in personal relationships. In helping others through this transformation she often asks and challenges her audiences with these questions: *Who are you? And if someone were to ask you to define yourself, what words would you use?*

She is awe-inspiring and a big-picture thinker who will teach you to think *big*.

Desiree Carter (Carter)
Thank you.

Wright
Can we trust God?

Carter

I believe this question deserves an individual opinion. We get to decide whether or not God is trustworthy. Instead of getting into some intellectual or theological diatribe, my answer instead is based upon my journey as well as my understanding of the human condition and God's interaction with me and my interaction with Him.

My understanding is that because of the human condition, trouble comes to everyone. It's in that trouble where we find ourselves between reconciliation and complaints or reconciliation and hope. It's between these elements that I find trusting God can offer a myriad of challenges. Some of these challenges take us on journeys that both ask and answer the question Can we trust God? The question is too profound to give the reader a simple yes; instead, it's all about looking at the journey, examining the heart, and sharing the decision to choose trust or become bitter.

When trouble comes, we often find ourselves asking God to explain His actions. God often answers with a cacophony of experience. These experiences often take us from death to life. They call us, challenging us to define ourselves. In defining ourselves, our attitudes and behaviors are developed based upon how we see or don't see God. Knowing how to live one's life is often based upon what we learn from these experiences. These experiences provide for us stories of relationship, heartache, moments of peace, struggle, and for the Christian, moments of love and hope.

Everyone has a story to tell. My story takes me from living in a shelter for the homeless, raising thirteen children—three of them biologically mine, nine of my children's friends, not to exclude one family member. I have survived having been emotionally, physically, and sexually battered by both spouses and a parent. I have survived the ridicule and fear of having become pregnant at the age of fourteen due to an unwanted sexual encounter.

I've lived through three divorces, custody battles, had children stolen and returned, and lived through threatening illnesses doctors could not explain. I've survived my own bad decisions and enjoyed the results of my good ones.

My ability to survive has not been under my own steam. As a child I didn't know God, but God knew me. God's grace carried me through a childhood of wanting to kill myself to challenging me as a young adult to care for and work with persons in prisons, mental health facilities, and persons suffering from alcohol and substance abuse issues. God has taken me from the corners of confusion to bring avenues of faith and strength. God has asked me to help others rediscover and reinvent themselves based upon who He says they are—made in His image.

Someone recently walked up to me and said, "Pastor, I'll bet you've never experienced anything bad in your life. You are so easy-going."

When I heard that, all I could do was laugh. I grew up believing Trouble was my first, middle, and last name. I thought that if one were to look up the word "trouble" in the dictionary, my face would show up. Many have often called me a modern day Job. Our stories are similar. My soul has always resonated with the story of Job and his misery. But don't take my word for it, read parts of it for yourself.

Staring at my Cola as though it had some life-giving power, my mind reeled with the memories of the past. I took another sip and remembered that death and life are connected—always intertwining like two star-crossed lovers' hearts. It was almost as though I could feel the force of yesterday; like bumper cars it bumped against today—the first encounter. Dodging his fits became an art form. Like pillows my cheeks embraced the strength of his hands, my teeth shifted, my jaw snapped, my neck spiraled out of control. My heart raced searching for excuses, wondering where God was. My eyes faded to green. Fear is the color of green.

For five years he used threats and beatings, using my own sense of poor self-esteem, and promises of death to keep me quiet. This pastor, this man of God used promises of annihilation and death to my children to keep me with him. It's hard to smile at others while knowing you are a hostage in your own house. It's even worse when trying to get away, knowing that any minute you're going to be the next headline in the news: "Mom and kids found dead on road" or "Mom kills pastor husband and sentenced to life in prison."

Taking another sip and stirring the ice, my heart began to feel frigid, afraid, almost as though I was still living the experience. Our apartment was cozy, on the second floor. We moved while he was at a pastor's conference. My children and I would be safe—at least for the night, I hoped. This would be the first night's rest I'd had in years. I played with the kids gave them a bath and put them to bed. The time was around nine o'clock. I stepped out of the shower, with fear dripping off me. I convinced myself it was safe to go to sleep. He couldn't possibly find us, I reasoned. Even my parents did not know where we were. And then it happened, midnight came and with it death.

"Hello, so here you are," he said.

I slowly sat up, watching the movement of his hands and body.

"You don't think you're going stay here—do you?"

In his usual authoritative tone, he suggested I wake the kids up and we all load into the car and go home. I don't know how he got in the apartment—I don't know how he found us. But, he promised to kill the kids if we didn't come back.

He was a man of the Gospel—a pastor—and I wondered how he could treat us with such disdain. He was my second husband. We were supposed to be safe with him. But he had taken everything from me, including my dignity.

When people think of death they think of it coming in a physical form. But death can come in diffcrent ways—emotionally and spiritually. I thought there was nothing else he could do to me; but I was wrong. Someone said when death comes it comes in threes.

It had been a month since my nose had captured the smell of her skin. I called, he said, "Tell me you love me and you can have her back.

My heart choked as the words flung forward, as daggers from my eyes they permeated the atmosphere. I choked silently on those words, "I love you."

"If you really want her back, meet me in Columbus," was the reply.

Columbus was an hour and a half away from where I lived. I had never been there before. He told me to meet him at a restaurant.

"Where is it"? I asked.

"You'll figure it out," he retorted. "You're smart. And by the way, if you're not there in an hour, she won't be there."

With that he hung up. My concern was that it was an hour and a half journey. My heart was terrified. I would miss the opportunity to take her home. However, he hadn't fulfilled his terrorizing quotient for the day—he was sitting in his car when I arrived.

She was sitting in the back seat pounding on the windows, screaming my name: Mommy! Mommy! As the steam from each drop of water burned holes in my heart, my heart screamed, "Give her back!" Although my vision was obscured by my tears, my eyes spied a brick on the ground, my brain told me to pick it up, throw it through the window, and snatch her out of the car. My soul immediately said, "No, she'd get hurt." And then I heard my tongue say, "She's only nine months old. Give her back!"

Then her eyes—red—connected with mine. His eyes met ours and then he said, "Take her."

Sometimes our experiences in life look as if they are our undoing, but, God is a God of justice and of grace. God is a God of death and resurrection, of love, and of promise. Throughout my life there were many experiences that shaped and molded me. When I look back, I realize God has used my experiences so that I might provide others with a grip of hope, offering them compassion and helping them to explore the way out of trouble.

Wright
What is the definition of faith?

Carter
When defining faith I look to the plaque that sits on my desk that says: "Faith is not knowing God can—faith is knowing He will." I don't know who created the saying, but it guides me. This plaque reminds me that God will and can change any negative circumstances into positive ones.

I was a group home administrator when God placed me in a shelter for the homeless. Being the only person with a bachelor's degree, a job, and married caused me to feel extremely embarrassed. Wondering why God would allow such a thing to happen to me, I soon found out.

Sometimes we think it's all about us; but rather, it's about what God can do through us. While living in that shelter, God allowed me to become acquainted with a couple of the women—one who was younger with a child and one who was older with two children.

The younger one was about to turn down a job because she didn't have the correct shoes, I heard her story, my heart was moved. I bought her shoes for her. She took the job and we were all elated. Soon she would be able to find a place to live and leave the shelter.

The second story has to do with a woman who hadn't worked for over twenty years. She had great compassion and was skilled in the art of taking care of others. My clients needed her. I asked if she was interested in working for me. There was an obstacle: she was on public assistance and her friends told her she would be crazy to give up the public assistance. They didn't know me, so they didn't trust me. But, she did and within a month she was working for me, at first part-time, then full-time. Later she went on to work for the county. We laughed about that, I had been trying to get a job with the county for months.

I soon realized my purpose. God's plan was for me to have met these two women and to use my influence to help them. As soon as I heard the Holy Spirit tell me this, someone told me of a house for rent. My children and I moved out of the homeless shelter. It was then I began to understand that faith means living in the shelter of God's love. Faith means believing in the power of a God who not only asks us to wait on Him, but to trust Him in the waiting. Faith has always clung to me, even when I am tempted to let it go.

Wright
What are some of the Bible images of faith?

Carter
My favorite character is of course a male character—David. David was a victor through Christ starting when God chose him as a young man to win all types of battles. One of the things that stand out for me is that David was very obedient to God; even when he messed up, he knew where to go back. He would always go back to God.

The other images for me have to do with two women. Mary, Jesus' mother, was very strong. She was a young girl who encountered an angel who told her she would be carrying the Lord. She didn't skirt from that. She could have run, she could have said, "Are you crazy? I am not going to do this. This takes a lot of work and I am too young. You are talking about having a child without having a man. That is going to get me in trouble with Joseph and his family." Instead she was very obedient. She stepped out on faith, listened to God and she followed.

My other person is Jezebel. She is a prime example to women of what we should not be. Wielding her beauty and power, Jezebel usurped her husband's authority in an attempt to destroy God's altars and kill His prophets.

If we're not careful we can develop a Jezebel spirit believing and acting as if beauty, money, power, and prestige are all that matters in life. We can use these God-given gifts to dazzle the world, wielding these gifts as dangerous swords, making them our god. We can get used to people lavishing attention on us because of what we have instead of who we are. If we're not careful, the power will go to our heads and define us according to the world's standards.

Jezebel's world told her she had more power than God. When God showed up, her beauty, her power, her prestige, and her money waned.

At her death Jezebel asked her gods, "Where are you now that I need you?" She talked about having given them allegiance and their payment to her was silence. She'd had faith in them. It wasn't until the real God showed up when she realized that she was in peril.

I can almost hear Jezebel say, "Don't follow my example because my example will lead you straight to the dogs."

Wright
How do you hang on to your faith in the midst of tragedy?

Carter
I'm human so I'll tell the truth; I cry, talk with God, and wait. God has never forgotten me. Even when I didn't know him, He knew me. He called to me, cradled me, guided me, and loved me in spite of me. In the midst of tragedy I realize there is a lesson either to learn from or to provide for someone else.

Here's an example. It was the fall of '83; I knew that trouble would show up, that "he" would come after me. He wasn't through torturing me yet. So as I walked out of my place of employment with a colleague and a group of developmentally disabled clients "he" drove up. I told my colleague to take my keys and either go back inside or drive away now. Not sensing the danger, my colleague didn't move quickly enough. Without a word "he" drove up, got out of his car, and punched me in the face. As my colleague stepped forward, "he" used his arms like tentacles and began choking me. His arms wrapped around my neck and squeezed.

My eyes began to fade to black.

I escaped but I knew I'd lose my job. God stepped in, however, and fixed even this. Instead of firing me the director of the company said, "You know we can't let you come back to this facility," she said, "but don't lose heart. We have a position opening up. If you'll take a weekend live-in position for a couple of months with the same benefits, full-time, I'll be able to offer you that position. By the way, it's a group home administrator's position. You've worked well for the company. We won't leave you stranded." God used her to help relocate me to another city and enabled me to still feed and clothe my children.

In the midst of this and many other tragedies faith has hung on to me. God has guided me, loved me, protected me, and given me a sense of hope. The Holy Spirit was my advocate even in the midst of the most dangerous situations, refusing to let me go. I'm really grateful that God saved me even before I knew I needed to be saved.

As a young person, my life was always unmanageable. God would always step in and take my life from chaos to joy—the joy of helping single moms, working with troubled teens, working with persons convicted of crimes, working with families in need of knowing they can make it through continues to be my call, and teaching others the importance of loving God, knowing that their help will come from Him.

I made a decision a long time ago to be a victor and not a victim. My entire life has been one training camp for learning how to deal with tragedy. Every day I spend time with God, putting myself under God's power and authority. Time spent with God helps me deal with life's present day realities and tragedies. My eyes and heart are fixated on the love that God personifies. My life is steeped and consecrated in prayer.

The voice of God reminds me that there is nothing too big for God to handle. There is no way for me to always make sense out of tragedies. So I do what my mother taught me: I don't forget in the dark what God has promised in the light.

Wright
What are some characteristics of faith?

Carter
I think one of the characteristics of faith has to do with trust. We get in our cars every day and we trust that our cars are going to start when we put our keys in the ignition. We don't have any problem with that. I think that sometimes, when we talk about trusting God in the midst of trouble and tragedy, we are not always sure God exists. Our relationship with God is mostly reactive as opposed to proactive.

We have faith in God as long as God is doing what we expect God to do, but if anything happens outside of what we believe to be the ordinary, our faith wanes. When we cannot describe or explain something in our lives, we begin to treat God like a spare tire, using Him and/or faith in the case of an emergency, until next time. The ability to trust has to do with building relationships and being in relationship with God. If we are going to be people of faith, we must read, study, and pray daily.

The other characteristic has to do with loyalty. Displaying loyalty is tough. Loyalty calls for one to walk in the light even when it's dark, especially when one doesn't understand the reason for the darkness. Faith asks us to walk in darkness expecting the light to show up even though you are afraid of the dark. God's promises are predictable in that they never change. God's promises cause us to walk in promises that find us in unlikely places. We may change, the seasons will change, but God's sovereignty never changes.

God is committed to love, loving us, being loyal to us, serving us, and encouraging us to be committed to Him and one another. God is a God of relationships, whether it involves relationships with other people or our one-on-one relationship with Him. God is a God of Hope. The characteristics of faith for me are: trust, loyalty, and commitment.

Wright

As a woman of faith, who does God say that you are?

Carter

As a woman of faith God says that I am powerful, loving, kind, compassionate, and willing to serve others without hesitation. God calls me to be wise, discerning, and knowledgeable in the pursuit of Him, living a life of love, hope, and forgiveness. I am a teacher who helps others redefine and reinvent who they are while looking at the image of God. My role as a woman of faith calls me to guide people through old tapes, providing them with steps that lead to emotional and spiritual wholeness.

My role as a woman of faith is to tell God's story.

Wright

What does it mean to be a woman of faith?

Carter

Being a woman of faith means having the courage to stand up for Christ. In standing up for Christ these women love more than others think is wise, and care more than others think they should. Being a woman of faith calls for one to love unconditionally, recognizing others' frailties as well as their strengths, and loving them anyway.

Being a woman of faith challenges me to recognize the importance of not just my own journey, but the importance of others' journeys.

Wright

How do women of faith meet the challenges of raising children?

Carter

Prayer, Prayer, and more prayer. My children have watched me struggle through life. Their struggle to believe in God has often been challenged by my life experiences, as well as their own.

The year was 1993. I was in my third year of seminary and my third marriage. Looking at our finances and knowing how tough it was for me to attend seminary full-time and work full-time, we agreed that I could quit my job and continue to attend school full-time. To seal my part of the deal I agreed to pay off all our current bills, except for the furniture and the utility bills. We could fall back on my savings account if we got into trouble. This agreement left us living off one check, which we could manage—at least until my graduation. However, two months later, my husband announced to me that he thought I should choose between him and God. I chose God; he chose to leave.

When he left I had no job, no transportation (our van had blown its engine), and thirteen children living with me. Within the next month our furniture would be repossessed. Losing our kitchen table was difficult, but losing our beds was the worst. The kids and I ended up sleeping on the floor (the floors were made of tile). So, I told the younger ones to act as though we were camping; we made pallets on the floor. The teenagers weren't happy and although some of their backgrounds had been rough, they were now used to the finer things in life. They wondered why, if I worked for God, God would allow us to live in such a manner. They wanted to know where God was. Secretly, I wanted to know too.

Someone in one of my church history classes had said that as students we qualified for assistance, and besides, we had been tax-paying citizens up until now.

In this situation, we quickly ran out of food, so I gathered up my self-respect and went to the welfare office. To add insult to injury, the clerk looked at me as though I was a cockroach. The woman sitting in judgment said, "You are a seminary student who gets student loans, you own a van, and you qualify for ten dollars per month in food stamps. In order for us to help you any more than that, you'll have to sell your van."

I said to her, "My van has no engine; even if I could sell it, how would I find work?" She looked at me and shrugged her shoulders. "Sell your van and we can help you," she repeated. I told her, "No, thank you," and walked out of the office.

It took four months for me to find a job. It didn't matter that I had two bachelor's degrees, had worked as a warden's assistant, and alcohol and drug counselor as well as a family counselor—everyone thought my skills were too advanced and I wouldn't stay with them. I was depressed and my kids were hungry.

Sensing my depression, my son asked me a question. "You are busy working for God," he said, "but Mom, what has God done for you lately?"

That question hurt because for the first time I realized I couldn't answer his question.

Women of faith teach their children that God is not in the business of creating chaos and confusion. In case you're wondering what happened, God sent someone who worked for a food pantry. They fed us for over six months. I found three part-time jobs—one was a job at a fast-food restaurant, one at a grocery store, and the other at a factory. Both my oldest son and I worked together to provide food for the family.

Women of faith use their sense of the Divine to create atmospheres where children are nurtured and have a clear sense of who they are and what they can do. They are affirmative in their talk with their children in every circumstance, guiding and teaching them to give thanks.

Wright

When it comes to relationships, how do women choose men of faith?

Carter

Creating and living in positive relationships is tough. It's work. Choosing a mate should be easy, but we often leave God out of the equation. Here are some steps that should be helpful:
1. Make sure you talk with God about the characteristics and traits you need in a mate. When asking God for a mate it's important for us to know what we're looking for. Asking God to help us see beyond the superficial is important.
2. Let God choose your mate. Get out of God's way. God knows who is good for you and who is not. Ask God and then wait. Remember he or she may not be the person you expected to arrive on your door step.
3. While you're waiting, take care of yourself, physically, financially, and emotionally. Don't come to the table with years of old baggage. If you know you need to lose weight (this goes for men and women), talk with your doctor, develop a plan, and commit yourself to action. If you know there are remnants of your past threatening to overtake

your future, go to a counselor—get some outside assistance. If you know your money is funny, you created the mess, the only one who can fix it is you.
4. Once your mate arrives, make sure you pray together. Go out together, doing things you both enjoy.
5. Don't function as if you are a married couple. Sex is sacred, it comes from God. It is a loving act—a physical and spiritual journey between two people.
6. If your relationship leads to marriage, remember to prepare for the marriage as much as you prepare for the wedding. Marriage can be tough. Marriage asks each person to put self aside, spend time with one another getting to know the needs, wants, likes, and dislikes of the other person. Communicate with one another, taking time to listen and talk. Share your ideas about marriage, and what it means to be a couple.

My husband and I have been married exactly one year. We love one another and know that God has placed us together. But, it's been a rough year. Within this year we have had to examine our understanding of who we are as a couple. We have had to examine who we are as individuals, and in the midst of all that, pull everything together so we function as one.

We haven't reached the pinnacle of oneness yet, but we're working on it. We have learned and continue to learn how our past relationships affect our present. We are learning how to speak one another's language, and continue to attempt to communicate in ways we both understand.

Early in our relationship we recognized that we each would not have chosen the other for ourselves; but God always has the last laugh—we are very much alike and just as different. The challenge for us is to not let our similarities or our differences get in the way of our experiencing the relationship God has ordained for us. We pray together, attend church together, and enjoy outings together. We look out for one another and we are one another's intercessor. It took six years for us to meet, become friends, lose one another, only to be brought back together. Our goal is to become one.

Before our marriage I had been alone for over ten years and it has taken some adjustment. We don't always agree, but we're learning and we're careful with not only what we say to one another, but also how we say things.

My husband is a man of faith. He is the head of the house, he honors me by making my feelings count, and he helps me laugh and cry. He is my lover and my friend. He is willing to take the time to get to know me—to understand me. He is learning what it means to love me as Christ loves the church. Is he perfect? No, but he is a God-send.

As we build a new life with one another, we are putting away the former things. We are people of faith who believe that God has led us to one another. Our goal is to make God proud while enjoying our lives together.

Wright
Do you think that premarital counseling is a good choice for couples?

Carter
I think that everyone should be involved in premarital counseling. Couples need to sit down and talk about and hear the real stuff. Premarital counseling gets us past the giddiness and the fluttering hearts. It provides an opportunity for couples to look realistically at what it takes to be a couple—two people who are now going to share everything. It's important to know how the other person handles situations in life.

Questions should be addressed such as: What part does religion play in your relationship? Who is going to discipline the children (if there are going to be any)? What is the couple's definition of marriage and love? How will the finances be handled and by whom? When angry, does one of you sulk while the other screams and yells? Does one or both of you use unfair fighting tactics—do you leave the room, expecting your partner to guess what's on your mind? These are the types of questions that are unveiled during premarital counseling.

Many people spend an inordinate amount of time preparing for the wedding, making sure the cake is just right, the dresses are perfect, the transportation, the pictures, reception, and honeymoon happen without a hitch. Musicians are hired, food is catered, the guest list is perfect, wedding planners are hired, the marriage license is paid for, the pastor is accounted for, and the rings are purchased. The couple can (if possible) spend an inordinate amount of money and time to make this event spectacular. Weddings are usually planned one to two years in advance.

Marriages aren't planned at all. Premarital counseling helps the couple plan the marriage.

Wright
What are your thoughts on women in ministry?

Carter
First, let me say that scripture does not prohibit women from being called to ministry. Women can serve in many different ways, including pastoring a church.

Second, I rarely get into dialogue concerning women's call to ministry. People like to argue. God is a God of supernatural powers and God is expecting His kingdom to be built by young and old, women and men.

As human beings we don't understand everything about God. I know some of us think we do, but we don't. When God calls us we have a responsibility to listen to Him and to do what He asks us to do. If rocks and trees can cry out, then certainly women can do that. If we read the scriptures honestly, God has been using and lifting women up for centuries. God can use whom God wants to. I don't think any human being has a right to question who God uses. If we read the scripture we find God using women in some miraculous ways. Mary was the mother of Jesus, Elizabeth the mother of John the Baptist, and Esther saved a nation. I'm not sure why there is so much dissention when it comes to women and their being in ministry, especially the pastorate. Women were the messengers God used to talk with the disciples after His resurrection. A woman was used to bring Christ into this world to redeem it.

As a female pastor I answer to God, not man. I know beyond a shadow of a doubt who called me. My job is to continue to be faithful in spite of what people think. If you're a woman and God has called you, answer Him. Let people work the issue out for themselves. You be faithful to God.

About the Author

DESIREE CARTER is an ordained pastor, author, keynote speaker, and workshop and seminar presenter who uses her skills of communication, behavioral modification, education, and her life's experiences to educate and empower others to succeed in business and life. Known as "the life force mechanic," she has over twenty years of experience challenging her audiences to look in the mirror and see the stranger within. She is a no-nonsense speaker who helps others sift through and unveil old paradigms that keep them from winning at life.

Talking with her audiences, Desiree challenges them with these questions: *Who are you? If someone were to ask you to define yourself, what words would you use?*

Desiree is a member of the National Speakers Association. She graduated from The Methodist Theological School of Ohio with a master's degree in Divinity and a master's degree in Alcohol and Substance Abuse ministry. She holds two Bachelor of Arts degrees, one in Vocational Rehabilitation and one in Sociology from Wilberforce University, in Wilberforce, Ohio.

Desiree Carter
Milford First United Methodist Church
541 Main Street
Milford, Ohio 45150
Phone: 513.831.5500
E-mail: DCarter478@aol.com

Chapter 10

CHARLDA SIZEMORE

THE INTERVIEW

David Wright (Wright)
Today we are talking with Charlda Carroll Sizemore. She brings to the world of Alzheimer's a unique perspective. She was married to her childhood sweetheart for thirty-four years. She learned firsthand the anguish of an Alzheimer's diagnosis. Her husband was the youngest individual in the state of Florida to be diagnosed with Alzheimer's. Her story traces their ten-year journey through the maze of denial and acceptance, love and frustration, tears and trials, so she would become the compassionate, devoted care-taker she aspired to be.

Her journey was not over when she lost him in 2001. Her beloved mother, soon after, began showing signs of dementia. This was once again a call to the challenge of providing love and support to a loved one in distress.

Charlda, welcome to *Remarkable Women of Faith*.

Sizemore
Thank you. I'm honored to be talking with you.

Wright

Great. We are honored to have you. What exactly is Alzheimer's disease?

Sizemore

Alzheimer's disease (AD) is essentially a breakdown in the functioning of the brain, but despite extensive research there is still so much we don't know. There are so many mysteries about it and that is unusual when you compare it to other illnesses. Someone with Alzheimer's can't retrieve certain information and therefore can't process information properly. He or she basically has certain information within the brain, but can't retrieve it. It can keep the brain from processing many specific types of information such as speech. Other difficulties include not being able to identify and use simple words, make decisions, or be able to use information to draw conclusions.

Wright

What is your interest in this disease now?

Sizemore

I feel a great deal of empathy for others going through similar experiences to mine and I want to provide some support and perspective for the secondary victims of Alzheimer's and dementia. I use the term "secondary victims" to identify the people who experience the rather complex collateral damage that this illness causes. People who are responsible for the victims of these diseases are unprepared and inexperienced due to the unusual nature of the disease.

When I think of my husband's early signs, I remember how difficult it was for me to know what was going on because there are no immediately noticeable physical issues. He just started changing his behavior. We stopped talking as much, and we stopped laughing and enjoying life as we used to. This felt like marital problems, not a physical disease. He wasn't diagnosed until several years later, so I spent all this time believing that my husband didn't love me as much as he used to. Then I found out that the behavior difference was a direct result of Alzheimer's. I struggled with depression for years while balancing the need to take the lead in the family as a caregiver. It was very hard and I now know that there is a need to support people going through what I went through.

It really wasn't until his behavior became so extreme that I even considered that we needed to seek medical advice. He started leaving doors open and disappearing, which was affecting his work. He was the headmaster of a school then and he would just suddenly disappear; nobody would know where he was. And as we later found out, even he wouldn't know. He started to use a notebook and write things down more than he used to. I know that doesn't sound unusual, but he had a fantastic memory and had never had to depend on written notes to remember things before. Then money would be missing and he would disappear for periods of time.

Friends and co-workers started noticing things, however, and when they mentioned concerns to me I found myself covering up for him, providing better excuses. I know now that it is a common reaction among caregivers. I thought that something was wrong but my pride told me that I could handle it—I could cover it up and make it right on my own. But really, I was just pretending that nothing was wrong.

My sister, Jill, was the only one I talked to about my concerns. As sisters do, she kept my secret and supported me. Thankfully, some wonderful friends of ours confronted me and forced me to acknowledge Buddy's problem. Johnny Schlechter, Buddy's long-time golfing buddy, noticed that he was using the wrong clubs when he was playing golf, saying strange things, and leaving car doors and trunks open. Johnny and his wife, Eleanor, and some other friends, the Walkers, confronted me and expressed their concerns. It wasn't until that day when I had the courage to find doctors who could help.

At first, not even the doctors expected anyone so young to have Alzheimer's. Buddy was forty-eight. Diagnosing his condition turned into a lengthy and arduous process. I finally found a family doctor who gave me a referral to a neurologist. Our GP was tentative at first because he could find nothing wrong with my husband. Buddy was so charming; he covered up his problems so well. But the doctor hadn't seen the day-to-day things that our close friends and I had seen. Our doctor gave me the referral and then Buddy was finally tested.

When we discovered he had Alzheimer's we found out that he was really in the late middle stage. This has always grieved me because medications such as Aricept are much more effective in the early stages. I struggled with guilt that I had not taken him to a doctor sooner.

I also want to honor my husband's struggle with the disease. Buddy and I were married for thirty-four years. He developed Alzheimer's at the age of forty-six, which is extremely young. He was the youngest man ever diagnosed with Alzheimer's at Shands Hospital at the University of Florida.

We associate Alzheimer's strictly with the elderly, but that's not always the case. We also dismiss it at times as a natural part of aging, which is very wrong.

My husband was a wonderful man, strong and good. He had a strong faith, loved God, and worked hard. Everything he put his hand to prospered. He took care of everybody. He was just a giant in everything he did. He went to Wake Forest University on a baseball scholarship, served his country as an Air Force pilot, helped build a family business, and even served as a headmaster at a private school. He had succeeded in every aspect of his life. He received the Distinguished Flying Cross while serving in Vietnam. Watching such a strong, proud man suffer so early in life inspires me to help others.

If I have a message for caregivers and for people who have concerns, it is to find out! Don't be afraid of knowledge. Knowledge is the greatest power we have. If I had known earlier what I know today, maybe things could have been easier.

Wright

What do you consider to be the greatest challenge to caregivers today?

Sizemore

First of all courage, followed closely by time management and planning.

Regarding courage, you have to face a lot of fear when dealing with Alzheimer's and dementia.

Regarding time management, you have to maximize your time because taking care of someone takes so much time that the other aspects of life can easily be mismanaged—finances, your own health, the other basics of life.

Regarding planning, you have to have plans for unknown complications that will arise—when the sufferer has extremely bad episodes, when your own health becomes a problem, when you need to work and your care-giving activities require attention. You have to plan for so many possibilities. It is a trying issue. The book, *The Thirty-Six Hour Day,* by Nancy L. Mace is an extensive look at how time management becomes such a difficult issue—you always need more time to do everything.

Wright

What do you think would be the best advice that you could give someone who has just received an Alzheimer's diagnosis for a loved one?

Sizemore

That there is a wealth of help out there. You are not alone. I think that there is a loneliness involved in being a caregiver and sometimes they tend to close gates and close themselves off from the world, to outside help, and to information and resources. There are wonderful organizations such as The Alzheimer's Association that have support groups for caregivers and can serve as valuable resources. You have to find people to help you. You cannot do it alone because that puts you and your loved one at risk. There are wonderful hospitals, there are wonderful doctors, and there are wonderful groups.

Another piece of advice I give is if the first resource doesn't work out, don't get discouraged and don't stop looking for alternative helpful environments. Keep looking to find something that helps you in your situation because everybody's situation is different.

Buddy was very young compared to most dealing with this issue, and I remember that the people in one of the first groups we attended together were much older than we were. That was hard for me and it made it difficult for me personally to relate. I kept looking and then I found a group with help and support through friends in the Alzheimer's Association. I found people who were in a similar boat—people I could relate to. I received a great deal of help, even if it just meant sharing and talking with others. I became friends with a woman who was also a caregiver to her husband, and our kinship helped me through all of it.

Wright

Statistics concerning dementia are alarming. Will you talk about that a bit?

Sizemore

Yes and I don't know exactly what the statistics are today, but I know that they are greatly on the increase. Dementia is a bigger, broader group. Alzheimer's is a form of dementia. Diagnoses have reached 20 percent in older age groups now and that scares us. There is a good reason: people are living longer. Buddy's early onset was very unusual. Alzheimer's is typically diagnosed when people are in their sixties and seventies. Alarmingly, it is diagnosed much more often today than ten years ago.

A lot of effort and money have been poured into research. As more and more people deal with it, more and more money has gone into research concerning Alzheimer's. Nancy Reagan has certainly been helpful with that. The statistics though are alarming and signal an increase, which encourages even more focus and more energy into research. This can bring good.

Wright

Is it different caring for a spouse than a parent?

Sizemore

Absolutely. A spouse, a partner, or a mother or father present different issues. One of the issues with my husband was that he had always been the driver of our car, but after he was diagnosed the doctor told me he shouldn't drive. When he was told he shouldn't drive, he still thought that he could—he wanted to get into the driver's seat and drive. When this happened, I had to learn a technique to change the way we had always done things.

We live in a world where truth is highly valued. Creating new truths is something you must learn to do with Alzheimer's patients. I "invented" the truth that I needed him to help me—to teach me how to drive because I was having problems driving. He had taught me how to drive when we were sixteen. I had to call on that long-ago experience so he would allow me to drive everywhere.

It was easy to get my mother not to drive. I would just say that I liked to drive her and that was fine. Parents tend to let you help them more than partners do. My husband tends to not want to give in to me for every decision. Parents are a little less that way. They see you as somebody they are expecting to supply their needs a little bit more. With a parent you have to really work at their being a unit with you more than you do with a husband. Your husband expects you to be a unit.

Wright

You touched on it before, but what is the difference between dementia and Alzheimer's?

Sizemore

Dementia is the broad term for neurological forgetfulness. Symptoms of dementia include forgetting, not being able to organize, not being able to fall asleep, and speech problems like not being able to find the right word, that sort of thing. Those are all cognitive issues—things we think about that go in the mind and we retrieve the information that has been filed away. Dementia can interfere with that.

Alzheimer's is one of the very extreme forms of dementia. Alzheimer's was named in 1907 for a German gentleman doctor whose name was Alzheimer. He isolated the specific symptoms of the disease that have more to do with the inability to function normally. It is a more severe form of dementia. Dementia is a broader term for things that everybody goes through with aging. It is a disease that is more manageable.

Wright

What were some of the first indications that your husband's health was threatened?

Sizemore

He started disappearing. He was working at the time. He had a wonderful job. He was the headmaster of a school. He would leave and nobody knew where he went. He had been a wonderful administrator and had hired exceptional people. They thought he was just busy and picked up the slack for him.

At home, he would take money and he would not remember where he'd spent it or what he had done with it. He was a very honorable and good man and that wasn't like him. I remember one day we drove together and he left me at school. He forgot that I was there and drove off without me. Fortunately we lived very close so I could just walk home. I walked in and said, "Buddy you left."

"Oh," he said, "I thought you were coming home with somebody else." He always had a very logical reason for why he did what he did.

The main symptom was forgetfulness. He was not thinking correctly. One time I was at a convention with him and he forgot I was with him. He went off to listen to a speaker in another room when I went around the corner to make a phone call. He never acknowledged there had been a mistake.

I look back on these things now and I don't know why I didn't see them more clearly than I did. If you don't know what these things can mean you don't evaluate them correctly. That is my goal today—I want to make people aware of the symptoms of Alzheimer's so diagnosis and help can come earlier. If people knew, they would recognize symptoms earlier and it would be less painful for both the victim and the caretaker.

Wright

What do you do after you've lost someone you love to a disease like Alzheimer's?

Sizemore

Alzheimer's takes up your whole life. It is just a gigantic task. Everything was focused on Buddy and everything was focused on my mom when they became ill. I thought constantly about what was best for them. I put them right up there at the very, very top of my priority list. Their death created a vast big hole in the center of my life.

Caretakers have usually given up every other interest in their lives. Rediscovering who they are is difficult.

The first two years I was numb. I had to find a way to fill the void with good things. God is so good. My first grandchild, Addison, was born six months after Buddy died. Two more grandchildren, Wake and Emmy Brooke, followed. They were like God's extreme kindness pouring out on me. They filled my life with such joy and reason for going on. The blessings they are gave me a reason to live.

You have to find a way to fill that hole with something good. It can be good work, people, or good actions. It takes time to find what the right calling for you is, but you must begin to see good and have a purpose again.

After the death of someone you love who had a disease as all encompassing as Alzheimer's, you need a little quiet time, a little healing time, and then you need a new purpose to pour your energy into. You need some time to be still and sort out your feelings. Then begin again. You want to give yourself a little rest and a little time. Soon you need to move past grieving and find something worthwhile to focus upon. I have observed those who give to another purpose do better than those who stay in grieving too long.

Encouragement from friends and family is vital. Often you cannot see your own reactions accurately. My family, my sister, Jill, my brother, Chip, and my sons, Trey and Brook, allowed me time to grieve and then encouraged me to get back into life. They propped me up and slowly let go, allowing me to stand on my own again.

I went back to teaching. I had been a teacher but had to stop. I stayed home and took care of Buddy for five years. The second year after he died, I went back to teaching, which was a wonderful thing for me. I found something I could do. I love my students. I am a reading teacher in a high school. Watching my students come alive to reading gave me a focus and a new joy for my life. It enabled me to go on.

Wright
Why are health issues for the caregiver so important?

Sizemore
You have to consciously think of it. As sad as this sounds, you need to think about what would happen if you died. A tremendous number of caregivers die before the person with Alzheimer's dies. It's way over 50 percent. It is a big concern. I discussed this issue with my children. I knew they would care for Buddy but I wanted to take the responsibility of making hard decisions away from them by making plans. I knew where Buddy would be taken care of well. I told people what should happen for Buddy if something happened to me.

You have to make plans about everything and being prepared is necessary for everyone's peace of mind.

Wright
How do you deal with family members who feel threatened by the very word "Alzheimer's"?

Sizemore
This is very common. I think the first thing you have to do is know that there will be people like this. There are people who step up to the plate and want to help you and who do help. There are also those for whom this issue is just too painful. They run away.

My husband was a very, very strong and wonderful man who had taken care of a lot of people. I was surprised at some of the people who couldn't come to see him. It was just too painful for them. I didn't comprehend this at first but I eventually came to understand.

God provided me with so many people who did stand by me through hard times: my sons, Trey and Brook, Buddy's father, my sister and brother, and lots of friends. Others who had been a big part of our life just couldn't be part of that part of life. You have to realize that it's not that they didn't love him—it's just that they couldn't watch someone they admired as strong seem vulnerable. It is a hard walk and everyone is not called to that walk. It was just too painful and too scary for them. God always provides what we need and there are always good people.

My friends and family were just wonderful to me. Johnny Schlechter had been Buddy's lifelong friend. He took Buddy to breakfast every morning for years. He and his wife, Eleanor, were strategic in getting Buddy to good doctors at Shand's Hospital. They were active in the daily care-giving needed to keep Buddy at home. Buddy's father came every day to help me and his aid was vital in helping me to manage money issues. Gloria and Edwin Lively prayed for Buddy daily. My sister, Jill, and brother, Chip, stood by me through everything. My sons became men and stepped into adulthood way before their time. Good can come out of terrible things. God gave my sons, Trey and Brook, strength and character—something that amazes me even today.

From the time Buddy was diagnosed, Trey, Brook, and my precious daughter-in-law, Holly, shielded me from all other conflict. They bonded to each other and found solutions to issues that Buddy and I as parents would normally have been able to help them with. They became rocks of faith and ability. God is good. I had grieved that they would not have Buddy to be their father in their teenage years and when they were in their early twenties. He had been such a wonderful father and he adored them so. They chose to let a handicap make them strong. Buddy is so proud of them today, I am sure.

My sister stood by me through the particularly hard times. Jill insisted I come and live next door to her when things got really intense. Buddy and I lived with my mother and she and Jill were there every day during really stressful times.

Buddy went through a little bit of an aggressive stage. He was never truly violent but he was rough. My sister, who is a little bitty person, was just wonderful. When the Alzheimer's Care Center found that Buddy was becoming too physical to stay there during the hours I taught at the community college, they sent their strongest male caregivers to help. Buddy would get angry and the men would leave hurriedly, promising to pray for us. Jill stood right with me. She was never afraid as others were. She never questioned my decisions. She just stood with me. If you are the friend of a caregiver you can use my sister as a model. She was there, always, whenever I needed her.

Wright

What were some of the unexpected reactions to your husband's health dilemma?

Sizemore

I think the avoidance. We must be prepared for the fact that some people just can't handle interaction with those who have Alzheimer's. I was surprised at that. But it is just too tough for some people and they really just can't handle it. It is important to release them and help them not feel guilty.

God always provides help. Sometimes it doesn't come from the people you expected, but God always meets our needs. Just understand that some are not called to this walk. They serve God and their fellow man in other ways. I always had the help I needed. Sometimes it just didn't come from the expected source.

Wright

What did you say when someone you knew asked casually how your mother was or how your husband was doing?

Sizemore

That's a hard question and people don't mean it to be difficult. They want to be supportive and they think they are being supportive, but "how is he [or she] doing" is a hard question to answer because with Alzheimer's, things usually get worse. People with Alzheimer's go downhill. It's not easy. It is sad to say but Alzheimer's is such a progressively negative disease, that question is not comfortable for the caregiver to answer.

Wright

Concerning hope, what does new research tell us about this disease?

Sizemore

A tremendous amount of research has been conducted. Huge amounts of money are being poured into Alzheimer's research. We thought we had a cure very recently. Researchers were feeling very positive about it, but it didn't work out. The side affects were extreme and so they moved on to look at alternatives. The answer is still being sought. In North Carolina big research centers are devoted to it. I believe that we will eventually find a solution.

We have learned more about the brain in the last twenty years than we ever knew before. We used to believe that people were born with a specific IQ and that's what they lived with. We used to believe that there are two IQs: math and verbal. Now we know there are at least fourteen different areas of IQ such as music and intuition. I believe all the information on how the brain works will lead us to a cure. We know that Alzheimer's affects and stops activity in parts of the brain. The fact that we know so much more about how the brain works makes me confident that we will find a solution—I know that we will.

Wright
Some people dread the thought of Alzheimer's and they overly react to such common things as forgetting a telephone number or the name of someone they've not seen in a long time. Is this cause for concern?

Sizemore
No, it's really not. We all have this kind of reaction. We all do that. It is not an indication of Alzheimer's. As a matter of fact, if we worry about forgetting something, we probably do not have a cognitive disease.

When the psychologist and the doctor made the final diagnosis, Buddy did not have a negative reaction. When we were questioned about our concerns, I was full of anxiety but Buddy was not the least bit concerned about it. He said the most amazing thing—he said, "I have a God who loves me and He's strong enough for this." I wrote that on lots of pieces of paper and taped them everywhere. I know it is true. We do have a God who loves us. He *is* much stronger than this disease.

Buddy had lived a life full of faith. He flew F4 and A7 aircraft during the Vietnam War and he was a heavily decorated veteran. He won the Distinguished Flying Cross and was the Top Gun of his squadron. So many people came to me after his diagnosis and told me amazing stories of kind and loving acts he had performed and had never told anyone.

Extremely intelligent people can get Alzheimer's. The great news is that it's not as difficult for the person who has it as it is for those who know and care for him or her. Alzheimer's patients are unaware of the changes. As caregivers we can wrap them in safety and love and enjoy the simple things of life.

Some wonderful friends, the Schlechters, took us to an appointment with the leading neurologist at Shands Hospital at the University of Florida. The doctor was a tremendous researcher. He was so wonderful to Buddy. I can remember once when he was examining Buddy, he asked him what a watch was. Buddy could not say what it was. He also asked him what my name was. Buddy did not know my name. He called me Darling and Sweetheart and that sort of thing for years but I did not realize he did not know my name.

Dr. Edelman was surrounded by young doctors and he sweetly looked at me and said, "I'll bet you know she loves you!"

Buddy said, "Yes, I do." That was a giant moment for me. He knew I loved him and he loved me. That was the important thing. No matter what else he forgot, I knew he knew I loved him.

Wright

What an interesting conversation. This is a terrible, terrible dilemma, isn't it?

Sizemore

It is a terrible dilemma, but you know, I have seen good come out of it. I have seen people in our family treat each other better, love each other more, value each other more, and live more in the present. God can bring good out of all things. I think it was Mark Twain who said, "Adventure is just a disaster rightly taken." And I think that's true. An adventure with Alzheimer's is not one I would have chosen but it is an adventure that our family was given.

The way Buddy died is not the totality of his life. He left behind great treasures. Alzheimer's did not win. It can be conquered. Buddy did that. I look at the strengths of his sons, Trey and Brook, and the evidence of the noble lives that are being lived after him. We need to be assured that good can come out of this. God can bring good out of everything.

Wright

Today we have been talking with Charlda Carroll Sizemore. She knows a lot about Alzheimer's. Unfortunately, she was married for thirty-four years to her childhood sweetheart when she first learned of his Alzheimer's diagnosis. Soon after his passing her mother began showing signs of the same disease. What a unique perspective and what a unique story Charlda has. She also has a unique opportunity now to help other people understand this terrible, terrible disease.

Charlda, I really appreciate your spending all this time with me today and answering all these questions. It's been enlightening for me.

Sizemore

Oh thank you so much. I have enjoyed this also. God bless you, David.

Wright

And thank you for being with us today on *Remarkable Women of Faith.*

About the Author

CHARLDA SIZEMORE brings to the world of Alzheimer's a unique perspective. She was married to her childhood sweetheart for thirty-four years. She learned firsthand the anguish of an Alzheimer's diagnosis. Her husband was the youngest individual in the state of Florida to be diagnosed with Alzheimer's. Her story traces their ten-year journey through the maze of denial and acceptance, love and frustration, tears and trials, so she would become the compassionate, devoted care-taker she aspired to be.

Her journey was not over when she lost him in 2001. Her beloved mother, soon after, began showing signs of dementia. This was once again a call to the challenge of providing love and support to a loved one in distress.

Charlda Carroll Sizemore
50 Eleventh Avenue #101
Indialantic, Fl 32903
Phone: 321.733.5542
E-mail: charldas@aol.com

Chapter 11

MARIA MULLEN

THE INTERVIEW

David Wright (Wright)
Today we're talking with Maria Mullen, a professional speaker, certified trainer, and Christian evangelist. She has a true passion to inspire, motivate, and equip people for success. Maria has spoken to adults and young people across the United States and Canada with her life-changing messages. She has personally used faith to overcome many obstacles in her life to become the successful person she is today. Maria is a member of the National Speakers Association and she is married with two beautiful daughters.

Maria, welcome to *Remarkable Women of Faith*.

Maria Mullen (Mullen)
Thank you, David.

Wright
You've been a corporate trainer for over a decade. How did you start motivating people through professional speaking?

Mullen

Well, as a trainer I enjoy the ability to help people grasp information and concepts easily. It allows me to flow in my creative zone and come up with techniques to help learners go from "deer in the headlights," to an "ah-ha" moment. But though this is a very fulfilling career, I felt that through professional speaking I could go beyond the formal classroom environment that focused on professional development and get more into human development on the personal level. I have had so many life experiences and lessons that I could put into programs that would help other people to be empowered to take their life to the next level.

Wright

What drives you to do what you do?

Mullen

Throughout my life I've met a lot of people who are living so far beneath where they could be. I discovered the power of the spoken word and how it can empower people to look past their obstacles and see opportunities. My passion is not found in the pocketbook (dollars), but it is found in people—seeing people break away from their fears and their limitations, accomplishing their goals, and walking in their destination drives me.

So many times it's just one word that can pull someone out of his or her box and into a place of extremes—and I love to see that!

Wright

What were some of the obstacles you had to overcome by faith?

Mullen

My biggest obstacle was fear! I think that's why many of my seminars address this issue in some format. I often tell people that if you look at the word "fear" you see the word "ear" inside of that word. This is a reminder that it is what you *hear* that can either fuel or extinguish the power of fear in your life.

I had to learn how to quiet those fear voices that kept me from taking chances and risks in my life, then turn around and listen to the power of faith. That's how I was able to achieve so many accomplishments in my life.

I also had to stop blaming circumstances like my lack of money for many of my challenges. This is why I produced my CD, *Money is*

Never the Problem. The information in the CD came from my life lesson about how we can focus so much on what we don't have (like money) that we start thinking in impossibilities instead of possibilities.

Wright
Why do you feel it's important for people to have faith?

Mullen
We live in a world where people have become so accustomed to facts and figures. If the numbers don't add up on paper or if the information can't be proven, it's hard for people to have confidence in themselves or to take risks in life. The reality is that sometimes things are not going to make sense; but somehow life has a way of making things come together. Even the Bible says in the book of Hebrews (chapter eleven, verse one) that, "Faith is the substance of things hoped for, the evidence of things not seen"! Imagine a world without faith—that world would be boring and limited because no one would make a move until "all the dots lined up."

How many times have you heard someone say, "I have a feeling it's the right time?" or "I don't know how this is going to work, but I'm going to try it anyway"? Well, that's faith because they are depending on something that is unknown. Businesses are created by faith, homes are built by faith, and families are created by faith. Why? Because in each case, nobody really knows the outcome of that dream or vision, but he or she steps out anyway. That's why it's so important that we *do* practice living by faith!

Wright
Someone was telling me the other day that he and his wife were going to wait until they had enough money and everything was in place before they had children. Now, if I had done that I wouldn't be the happy daddy I am today!

Often people refer to faith in a religious context. Do you feel that people have to believe in God in order to have faith?

Mullen
No, because everyone practices faith without even thinking about it! How many times do you sit down in a chair without checking to see if it will hold you up? Well, you just *believed* that the chair would hold you up without proof. This is a form of faith. There are many

things we just believe in without the evidence in front of us. Even that Scripture I quoted in Hebrews never mentioned faith in "God," it just said, "faith is the substance of things hoped for"!

See, faith is nothing more than holding on to the thing you can't see while waiting for the thing you are hoping for to happen. Wow!

Now, for spiritual or religious people, that "thing" happens to be the power of God, because God represents a power that they can trust in when they can't see the possibility through their own power. When what you desire is beyond your ability, you trust in another power that can work on your behalf. For example, I hear people say they put their trust in the stock market in order to become wealthy—that's where they put their faith, that's where they put their belief—the power of the stock market. I personally put my faith in God because He is a power beyond my own. How could I fail with God as my guide?

Wright
Why do you think some people find it challenging to use faith in their lives?

Mullen
People tend to have a hard time with the unexplained. They have a hard time accepting things that don't add up, or "make sense," so faith seems crazy to them. There's a need that humans have to believe in the tangible things of life rather than in the unknown. Look at the television show *The X-Files*. The female character, Scully, had such a hard time thinking the recurring unexplained phenomena had anything to do with UFOs. She was always trying to logically explain situations even though the situations defied all logic.

The more knowledge we acquire, the more we feel that we need to have the answers to situations in our lives. Faith, unfortunately, doesn't always have the answers and sometimes there isn't anything tangible to touch—you just have to believe!

Wright
Who are some of your personal role models?

Mullen
There are so many, but two who come to mind right now are both my parents, Sam and Bea Brown. They both came from challenging childhoods. My mom's father was killed in a car accident when she was only two years old, and her and her twin sister had to be given

away to family members. They never grew up with their own mom, yet my mom has turned out to be the most loving and giving and strong mother to our family in spite of her childhood challenges. She's the one who has shown me how to sacrifice for others. She showed me how to make a home filled with love, life, and laughter. Her faith and creativity are strong; she actually was the one who led the whole family to faith in Christ.

My dad lost his mom as a teenager to breast cancer, and shortly after that his dad was killed on the side of a road while changing a tire. So he ended up going into the military and serving in Vietnam. He had many challenges in his life, but in spite of those challenges he ended up being a *great* dad, bringing an awesome balance of strength and sensitivity to the family. He also has the best sense of humor. He's a great leader, and he's taught us the importance of family and life values. This man has a way of looking into the deep and sentimental areas of life and showing an appreciation for things most people look past. Not only that, but he took time to support my activities and my brother's activities also.

My parents taught us to value people, not things. I guess that is why I am so people-centered and not driven by the dollar sign. Together my parents provided a healthy environment for the family that has allowed me to grow into the person that I am today—so I'd say that they would be the top role models in my life! Not many people can say that these days.

Wright

Would you tell our readers two or three things they can do to begin to achieve their path of success?

Mullen

Yes—Confront, Conquer, and Create. I look at life as a builder who has a dream to build. We all have dreams and we all have goals of success, but just like a builder you have to first survey your land, and that land represents your life. You have to look at your life and you have to see what currently exists in your life. You then have to determine how to build that dream into your life. In other words, *confront* your existing issues: What habits do you have to change? How is your thinking affecting your dream? Who are the people on your team? What current problems do you have in your life? What have you been running away from all your life? What are your fears? These are the types of issues you have to stop and confront before you go into creating your dream.

Second, just like a builder you have to remove or *conquer* the things that might be on the "land" of your life that can hinder the building process. Everything you confront in your life doesn't necessarily have to be removed—just addressed and recognized. But there are some things in your life that must be removed in order for your dream to happen. Again, evaluate your life: Are there toxic people in your life? Do you live in a poor environment for growth? Is there debt that must be removed before you can go forward?

Finally, once the "clean up" process has been completed, then you need to prepare yourself for the building process. Creating your dream doesn't mean just jumping in with both feet and saying the sky is the limit. You have to take it step by step and try not to abort the journey just to reach your destination.

I teach women about creating their dreams in my *Reinvention of Me* conference I held in January. It's fun to see the women actually build their dreams like a builder. Many discovered that they had been taking too many big steps that discouraged them along the way. Sometimes it just means taking smaller steps to make a dream happen.

Wright

How would you suggest that our readers stay motivated when circumstances seem bleak?

Mullen

I would say that the key is to stay focused on positive results and not to focus so much on negative obstacles, then you'll reach your goals. See, sometimes we focus so much on what is going wrong that we get disoriented. Your motivation is going to come from what you have the ability to *do* with what you *have* where you *are*, and the rest actually comes by faith.

In my life, every time I come upon a challenge, I ask myself, "What *can* I do?" Oftentimes it is so easy for us to make of list of what we can't do and what we don't have. Dreams are exciting and sometimes that excitement causes us to take big steps just because we want to hurry up and get to the dream. Well, sometimes we have to learn to slow down and take smaller steps toward our dream. The key is to keep moving. Even the Bible says the race is not given to the swift nor to the strong, but to the one who endures until the end (Ecclesiastes 9:11 and Matthew 24:13). If I had to sum it up into three words I would say: Faith, Focus, and Endurance are the keys to staying motivated.

Wright

What are some of your accomplishments that required faith?

Mullen

The biggest accomplishment was when I left ten years of being in the administrative field and stepped into being a corporate trainer, which was totally against my natural personality. I always was a shy person, so working behind the scenes was comfortable for me. I also wasn't very good with networking so hiding behind a computer and telephone was easy—but by faith I left that comfort zone and stepped into what I like to call a "Creative Zone." This new zone allowed me to do something I thought I would never do—being up in front of people and training. Once I realized that training was my calling, I then got the courage to accept my calling into the ministry. Oh, I was wide open by then so that's when speaking professionally came with ease.

The second accomplishment was when I first left my hometown of Springfield, Massachusetts, at twenty-one years old and moved to Baltimore, Maryland. This move took a lot of faith because even though I had a plan, there were times when I didn't actually *see* how certain things were going to work. I kept going anyway. It only took me six months to complete the process.

And then finally, in 2004, my husband and I purchased our dream house—a six-bedroom house on a lake. Literally, we woke up one morning and said, "We're going to get that house!" We were living in a house that we had had for seven years, and I just said, "Let's do it!" We had no money saved up and no planning; we didn't even have our own realtor and mortgage company lined up. But forty-five days later we were in our dream house. Everything just seemed to fall into place and we've enjoyed our little retreat ever since.

Wright

When you travel around and speak to different audiences, what unique value do you bring to them?

Mullen

I focus on giving people a blueprint—directions and tasks that they can use to, as my famous line says, "Maximize their life's potential!" I don't want to just inspire or motivate people, but I want to *equip* people with the tools they need for success. I try to be *real* with my audiences. I make sure that I'm always including information they can take away and do something with when they leave the seminar, and that they are not just sitting there in a cheerleading session.

Too many speakers focus on "wowing" the audience but then it ends up feeling like a cotton candy dinner—no substance. I believe in bringing uniqueness to the information I present. Let's face it—there are hundreds of speakers out there speaking on similar topics. I work hard to give my audiences substance—something they can draw on to keep them going on their life's journey. Additionally, much of what I talk about I've personally experienced, learned, or I know someone who has experienced it.

Wright

What are some of the biggest lessons you have learned in your life?

Mullen

That the mind is so powerful and has the ability to make or break a person's life! The power of a person's words, when put together with the power of the human mind, can affect our lives more than we can ever conceive. This is why it is so important that we control what we allow in our mind. I've learned how to change my mentality to change my life. Readers of this book will be empowered to make new steps in their lives just by what they read today.

As a professional speaker I have a great responsibility when I speak because I literally hold the lives of people in my hands. Seminars, workshops, keynote speeches, CDs, and books can all be life-changing for an individual. I take what I say very seriously. If we all learned how to change our mentality we could then change our world!

Wright

You've talked a lot about faith. I remember a wise man telling me many years ago, "David, if you were walking down a road and found a turtle sitting on a fence post, you can bet that he didn't get up there by himself!" Are there any people in your life other than your parents who were really instrumental in making you the person you are today?

Mullen

Yes, I have a best friend named Kenny Mays who has been such an influence in my life since he was fourteen and I was twelve. We are still friends today. He has been in my life with all his crazy ideas; he's always been there to say, "Yeah, let's try it!" He is actually the one who encouraged me to go into corporate training. Every time I reached a point where I didn't believe I could do something, he was there to help me change my mentality and believe in the impossible. When I wanted to step into professional speaking, it was Kenny who encouraged me to make the step. You talk about faith—he's definitely walking faith. So he's truly a significant person in my life.

Another person is Gayle Hendrix. She and I worked at Coca-Cola Enterprises Inc. together as instructors. When she found out that I was pursuing professional speaking she became my personal cheerleader. She always had an encouraging word for me and when I would get slack, she was right there to push me to keep going. Gayle even offered to edit my books and listen to my draft recordings when I would create various products. She gave me honest and constructive criticism to help me put out the best product. She wasn't a long-time friend or family member, nor did we work together very long, yet she showed me more support than many of my inner circle friends. She had the best sense of humor and always kept me laughing. I don't know if she even realized how much of an impact her support meant to me.

Wright

As you look into the future, what's it in for Maria Mullen?

Mullen

What's in the future for me is to accomplish the dreams that are in my head. I have big dreams of making a difference in society. I want to leave that kind of legacy. I don't care much about a lot of money to buy big fancy houses, cars, clothes, and diamonds. I want enough money so that I can continue to use the gifts that God gave me to empower people to live their lives to the fullest. If I can empower a child to become the next president, even though that child grew up in the ghetto with little education, then I am successful. If I can empower a single mother to own her own home and start a business, then I am successful. If I can empower an abused woman to see hope and recreate her life again, then I am successful. If I had the resources to give low-income neighborhoods the same schools, housing, and employment opportunities as middle- and upper-class neighborhoods, then I am successful. For me, it's not about me—it's about seeing a generation where success is redefined to mean more than the accumulation of things, but about the value of individual people and the gifts they have to offer back to society.

Wright
No wonder you are so successful, you are very interesting and I really appreciate your spending all this time with me today answering all these questions. I think that you are helping people, and I wish you all the success in the world!

Mullen
Thank you very much; it's been my pleasure!

Wright
Today I have been speaking with Maria D. Mullen, and as we have found out today, her message of faith can be life-changing.

Thank you so much, Maria, for being with us today on *Remarkable Women of Faith*.

About the Author

MARIA D. MULLEN Has over a decade of diverse training experience both as a consultant and as a professional certified trainer for major corporations (Coca-Cola Enterprises and the American Cancer Society). Her national and international audiences have run the gamut from top executives, administrative support staff, professional staff and production employees to truck drivers. As a professional speaker, her life-changing messages have impacted many groups including: corporate teams, industry associations, youth groups, and church groups. She is not only a powerful motivator in person but she has produced several motivating CDs through her label, *Java Drive*. She is also completing several literary projects. Maria's mission is simple: to empower you to maximize your life's potential—to go beyond your comfort zone and into your creative zone.

Maria D. Mullen
Clear Steps Group
1415 Hwy. 85, Suite 310-103
Fayetteville, GA 30214
Phone: 877.293.2830
E-mail: Maria@SpeakMaria.com
www.SpeakMaria.com

Chapter 12

DeBee Trant

THE INTERVIEW

David Wright (Wright)
Today we're talking with DeBee Trant, founder of Up Close Ministries located in San Diego County, California. She and her husband, Michael, have dedicated this ministry to helping people of all ages develop stronger spiritual relationships with God through biblical teaching and outreach efforts. DeBee is a motivational Christian author and speaker. Through her own personal story and background she draws others into a more grounded and intimate relationship with Jesus Christ. She enjoys helping others learn to intertwine their personal lives with the Word of God and prayer to empower them to live joyful, victorious lives for Christ.

DeBee, welcome to *Remarkable Women of Faith*!

DeBee Trant (Trant)
Thank you, David, for including me as a "remarkable woman of faith."

Wright

DeBee, why don't we begin by having you share with our readers how Up Close Ministries came about?

Trant

Many years ago I started teaching on healing after serious marital issues had left me in a state of depression. In an effort to feel better, I attended an in-depth emotional healing Bible study. The study began helping me to "breathe again" and come out of the gray, hopeless place that depression is.

That study, "Lord, Heal My Hurts," about twelve years ago, was the seed for me to start teaching in-depth healing courses for Christian women. I felt called to Christian women because I knew that a lot of women in our churches were just like me. They loved the Lord with all their heart and they felt they were doing things right, and yet their lives were not what the Bible promises. Our upbringing and life experiences affect the why we interpret the Word of God. Following the crisis that I had been faced with, I knew that God was calling me to use my own life experiences in order to help other Christian women.

When doing public ministry, you do not always have financial support from others. Michael and I began to feel God calling us to create a 501(c)(3) or charitable organization as defined by the IRS. This has made it possible for others to support our efforts while receiving a tax credit for their support.

We now speak to groups helping them identify and concentrate the formula for healing. It is our desire to help others begin the healing process in a retreat or a workshop setting. There are a number of Christians today who are so busy and stressed out that the thought of a twelve- to fourteen-week study is an impossible challenge. It is our belief that God wants to use Up Close Ministries as a starting point in healing. As hope is received, individuals are given more long-term resources to use in their daily journey to emotional health and healing.

Healing is a lifelong journey. It is the desire of Up Close Ministries to equip others to use their lives and the power of the God they serve to minister to others in their communities and in their own churches.

Wright

Would you take a few moments to share with us the *statement of the purpose* for Up Close Ministries?

Trant

Up Close Ministries is based on *"spiritual truths that emotionally heal."* We believe that a large percentage of men and women in modern day churches today are emotionally in crisis. They are in crisis because of damage that was done to them, not only from their childhood or their parents, but also from the suffering that occurs as we live on the planet Earth. Many suffer from death and divorce, combined with situations that are unique in modern society.

Christians need Scripture that is specifically directed at emotional healing and used to address serious issues in life. Up Close Ministries takes God's Word and the spiritual truth in it to bring about emotional healing. When emotional healing takes place we allow ourselves to have a more intimate relationship with Jesus Christ. The truths that allow us to heal also provide a way for genuine friendship and trust with God. We will allow God to get emotionally closer than ever before.

Wright

DeBee, I've never met anyone with such an unusual name. Is this a special name that runs in your family or did your parents come up with it?

Trant

I was born into a very violent, abusive family, David. My mom and dad had twelve children and I was number six. When I was born I was named Deborah.

As I grew up and began to emotionally heal, I wanted to know why I was special to God. I did not feel special—I felt unworthy and dirty like a bad little girl. As I began to mentally mend I felt God calling me deeper into ministry. I asked God to show me why He wanted me. I knew that God didn't need me, He can take care of whatever He needs too without my help; but I desired to know why he wanted me to join Him when there were so many more qualified women to do the job. I didn't feel that I was worthy of being used by Him to help others.

I was driving my car and having this little talk with God in my mind. All of a sudden He showed me my name, and He re-spelled it right in front of me. God showed me, "You're not going to be Deborah anymore; you're going to be DeBee (pronounced 'Debbie')." Deborah means Bee in the Bible and "a seeker of truth," while Debbie in modern terms means "busy as a bee." My mother gave *birth* to a high energy little girl who always sought after truth, wanting to know "why?" My parents named me Deborah. God renamed me *DeBee*. He showed me what He had *birthed* in me. God planned who I would be before the world was ever formed—a woman who was busy seeking the truth according to the Word of God. In the Bible, God renamed many godly people, giving them new names. God gave me a new name. God told me that day that I was like a bumblebee. He asked me to begin encouraging others—to help them take the damage in their lives and turn it around into something good and use it to minister to others.

God showed me Scriptures that began to encourage me. *Judges 14:5–6a and 8–9a:* 5.*Samson went down to Timnah together with his father and mother. As they approached the vineyards of Timnah, suddenly a young lion came roaring toward him.* 6a. *The spirit of the Lord came upon him in power so that he tore the lion apart with his bare hands as he might have torn a young goat.* 8. *Some time later, when he went back to marry her, he turned aside to look at the lion's carcass. In it was a swarm of bees and some honey,* 9a. *Which he scooped out with his hands and ate as he went along. When he rejoined his parents, he gave them some, and they too ate it.*

Samson was fed along the way and he fed others. Out of something that was meant to destroy Samson, came something good instead.

Out of what Satan meant to destroy me, came healing instead. I hope to be like honey for those weak from life's journey, that they might be "strengthened" as they go along.

Wright

What is it you hope to change in peoples' lives when you accept an invitation?

Trant

We (Michael and I) want to give people hope. It's our desire that when people arrive to hear us they depart knowing they are not alone and that they know someone understands and cares.

Jesus Christ cares very much what we suffer and what we feel. He wants to put us back the way we were when He formed us in the womb—when He formed us before the foundation of the Earth. He wants to use the things of the Earth to refine us and to make us into the image of Himself. The world bends us and hurts us. God takes hurtful things and molds us into what He knows we can be. When people come to hear us speak, we want them to leave with hope and direction. Our desire is that they will not be satisfied with life the way it is after hearing what God has done for us and can also do for them.

Wright

DeBee, was there anything specific that happened in your life that was the catalyst to start you working on healing?

Trant

After witnessing my now ex-husband taking drugs and losing all hope of his recovery, I fell into a deep, dark, black depression. I had never suffered with any form of depression and didn't understand the hopeless feeling that accompanies it. I went into such a black depression that I couldn't smile, I found no reason to get out of bed, and I didn't care if I lived or died. I cried uncontrollably for hours. The color went completely out of my life. I saw a black-and-white world. I didn't want to take my own life, but I really didn't care if it ended the next day. My depression was difficult for others to watch. I had been a very happy and up-beat person—an A-type personality—and I immediately went into a very black, hopeless place. I lost weight rapidly and began to show the pain in my physical body.

A family member named Priscilla reached out and handed me, *Lord, Heal My Hurts,* and told me that a Bible study was about to begin. At that time I didn't want anything to do with it, but I still thought I had to prove that nobody could help me and that nothing would work—so I went to the Bible study.

The person who most helped me in my healing journey was Kay Arthur, founder of Precept Ministries. Her book, *Lord, Heal my Hurts*, began a foundational healing process that continues in my life today. Kay Arthur reached out into my life through the pages of that study. I was in a black, dark, depression and she helped me to crawl back up, out of the darkness. The Word of God, applied to my life, began healing many traumatic issues. I was able to unbend the things I had been taught as a Christian woman that were not correct. I will always be grateful to Kay Arthur and what she wrote in her books that helped me to feel happy and excited about life again.

That day God reached out to me in my darkness and hopelessness. He showed me how much He loved me. On that day the color began seeping back into my life. God began a work in me that has changed my life forever.

Wriht

Is there a place for humor and laughter in dealing with hurting people? How do you incorporate fun into your motivational messages and workshops?

Trant

We at Up Close Ministries believe laughter is medicine. It says in Proverbs 17:22, *"A merry heart doeth good like a medicine, but a broken spirit drieth the bones."* A cheerful mind works healing! Absolutely, we believe that there should be joy in the Lord! Healing allows joy to come into our life. We may be able to laugh more and be okay having fun. Life itself is funny, so enjoy it; become aware of it. Take the Word of God and apply it to some of the serious current life situations we experience; some of them can be pretty amusing. We can laugh in the face of the evil one as we become the joy-filled people God intended us to be. I recently had a laugh with the Lord over why he had me teach so many intense healing courses over and over for so many years. His answer to me? "Oh DeBee honey, it has taken *you* that many times to get it!"

We like to use visuals when we are invited to speak. We do funny things. One of our alter egos is Buzzzy Bee, and if you get on our Web site you'll see a picture of Buzzzy Bee—she does ministry with us at Up Close Ministries. Buzzzy Bee's purpose is to lighten the effects when speaking about abuse.

Laughter is healing; we can hurt and still enjoy life. The sun shines every day, and we can go out and feel its warmth, and appreciate all that God does, even though we may have had or have hurts and pains in our lives. As we heal we are able to see more of the good things that God is doing every day. We are able to welcome His blessings into our lives!

Wright

Will you share with our readers those who you credit with having had the greatest spiritual impact on you personally?

Trant

The number one person of course would be Jesus Christ. I received Jesus when I was thirteen years old in Houston, Texas, in a "fire and brimstone" church. That preacher talked about what would happen if I died that day. I already lived in hell but I thought, "You know, it could get a whole lot worse than it is today!" That day I received Jesus Christ as my Savior and everything changed from that moment forward. It didn't get me out of my earthly hell, but God showed me how to hang on through it and to have hope for the future.

The second person who has greatly impacted my life is my husband, Michael. When I met Michael he was a professional parade clown in addition to his regular day job. Michael was very funny and I was very serious. I learned from my husband what it's like to have a man who really loves you, cherishes you, and takes care of you. It was very healing to know that God brought him into my life. He taught me how to be silly; he taught me how to have fun in my relationships with others and in my relationship with Jesus Christ. He even got me involved in clowning. You can meet my alter ego Buzzzy Bee on our Web site if you like.

Wright

Would you share with our readers what you believe is critical in the process of forgiveness?

Trant

If you haven't learned to forgive it's creating damage. When we come to believe and accept that it is necessary and required by God, we can begin to heal by moving forward. In the Word of God it says that we are going to be forgiven to the degree that we forgive. Matthew 6:14–15: *"For if you forgive men when they sin against you, your heavenly father will also forgive you. 15. But if you do not forgive men their sins, your father will not forgive your sins."*

This can be a difficult thing for us to accept, especially if a close relative or friend has abused us. Many would say, "You have a right to be angry; you have a right not to forgive." That's not true! The truth is that the Word of God says that we *have to forgive*, and that *if* we forgive we will also be forgiven.

Through the study of the Word of God and prayer, we become able to finally release our anxiety and our hurt over what someone has done to us. We are strengthened and empowered to give it to God. We begin to understand that we can trust Him to take care of it. When we give it to Him, He is able to do far more than we can. He is not happy about what has happened to us. It makes God angry when people don't listen to Him, and that's how sin occurs—when people don't listen to God. When we don't listen or the person who hurt us has not listened to God, we can trust God to handle it so we can move on with our lives.

A story I often tell when I am teaching on forgiveness is the moment when God helped me to release my hate toward my father. I was driving and thinking about how much I hated him and talking to God about it. God said to me, "DeBee, what would you like me to do to your dad so you can feel that he has paid the debt he owes you?"

I replied, "Put him in hell for twenty-five years. That would be enough to pay for the damage he has done."

Jesus said to me, "DeBee honey, I can't do that, it's eternity or nothing. Do you want him to go to hell for eternity?"

At that same moment I realized from studying the Word of God that I also deserved hell for eternity for the sins I had committed in my life and that if my dad deserved hell for eternity so did I. It became clear to me what God meant in his Word. Sin is sin to a holy God. Humans categorize sin, hold on to it, and cling to the events and pain so that it validates it somehow. That is a lie of Satan, a half-truth to hold us in our own human hell on Earth.

I replied to God (a little disgusted), "Well, if he deserves it so do I. I accept your forgiveness and release from punishment. I will also allow my father to receive the same gift. No, I do not want you to send him to hell for eternity."

I allowed God to do His job that day and I took my hands off. My job was not to punish but to forgive. I felt a great burden lifted that day in my car and a deep healing began to permeate my being for the first time. I experienced a new level of obedience and commitment to God. I did not have to *fully* understand to trust and obey.

Had my father continued in sin, not listening to God and hurting people until his death in 1994, he would have ended up in hell for eternity. It would have been a trip of his own choosing, not because I sent him there. If we will study the Word of God, it will empower us to release. Getting involved with studies that teach about forgiveness is a key to true, long-term emotional healing.

The day I forgave my father was one of the most revealing days of my life. I was eaten up by self-righteous hate the day God led me into releasing and forgiving him. I am grateful to God for showing me, through the study of His Word, why I was wrong, and how to stop holding on to pain. Forgiveness is a critical necessity for emotional healing. I had the honor of leading my father to the Lord on his deathbed and look forward to seeing him again someday in heaven. I look forward to seeing my father, not as the man he was, but as the man God always wanted him to be—a man who will listen and obey God, loving God with all his heart, soul, mind, and strength.

What is critical in forgiveness? Study of the Word, prayer, and obedience to what God tells us to do. We must try to forgive those who have hurt us. God will make it possible for us to accomplish. It can be done! It will profoundly change our relationship with a long-suffering, loving God. Study of the Word will empower us to do some very hard things in our spiritual development . . . forgiveness is one of the hardest.

Wright
Is forgiveness necessary for healing? Can't we just forget about it?

Trant
We can't forget about it. It's always in there. We might think that we can shove it down, but we end up not being as full of joy, we may not feel quite right, not happy. We don't even realize that we're not—we get so used to feeling the way we've always felt—and shutting down is just an integral part of who we have become. Once we learn to let go of it, we will find forgiveness is critical to having an intimate relationship with Jesus Christ. Sometimes that word "intimacy" scares us, and it scares us because we are afraid of it. Sometimes childhood events make us fear intimacy. Intimacy with God is a wonderful thing; it's like a really warm hug (with no sexual overtones) from somebody you really love and trust.

If we shove down our pain, we also shove down forgiveness. Maybe we think it's too hard, or we just don't feel up to the work of trying. The pain will sit inside of us for the rest of our life. The pain we hold on to gives Satan a place to hold onto us, keeping us captive and unable to do and receive many of the deeper spiritual teachings and healings of God.

God will love us even if we never can forgive those who have hurt us. He will receive us into heaven—He loves us—He just doesn't want us to suffer! He wants us to be happy and He wants us to be full of joy. He wants us to be able to receive His greatest gifts. To do that we will need to trust him and walk in obedience.

Sometimes that obedience is simply believing and beginning. We may be surprised at the results that God can bring about in our life. Is it possible that we could experience His love and forgiveness more fully? Is it possible that we could be happier tomorrow than we are today? Are we able to accept and feel deep, joyous love from God to us? Daniel 11:32b says this: *"But the people who know their God shall be strong and carry out great exploits."* I believe one of those exploits we can carry out on His behalf is the ability to forgive.

Wright

Do you believe people who are recovering from the trauma of life—especially deep childhood damage—can ever hope to feel normal?

Trant

The word "normal" is an odd word. Many people today would say, "Is there really a 'normal' anymore?" If you look at some of the synonyms for the word "normal" we might feel the need to be "like" everyone else. I encourage others to resist the word "normal" and to embrace the word "unique." God made us to be unique.

Most of us are searching for a unique relationship with the Lord. We want Him to show us why we are special. The "normal" people who have a hard time feeling God's presence are in a box. We've all heard the term "think outside the box." I encourage others to think outside the box to become who they are really meant to be. We were not created to be clones of each other.

My children and I laugh about how we are not normal! We are not normal and I love it that my children are not normal. We are abnormal and we enjoy the thought of that. My husband, Michael, likes to say he is the most normal one in the bunch. When you meet Michael you will realize what a joke that is. Like the rest of us, he is special in a *wacky way.*

The way I use the negative things that happened to me as a child and openly share them when I minister to others may appear abnormal (not normal). To God it makes me special and unique. I have a unique task that God has set before me; not all are called with this purpose. I am comfortable speaking about things that many other speakers are not. I share what it's like to have a violent dad as well as to experience abuse as a child. Because I have experienced these things personally I understand what they can do to Christian thinking.

I'm not normal, and God does not want me to be normal. God wants me to be unique. He wants us to embrace our special, unique lives and personalities and bring them to Him to be used for His glory. These are things that Satan wants to destroy us with and we are given the power through our faith in Jesus Christ to give them back to God to be used for His Glory—for good and not for bad. My life verse is Revelation 12:11: *"They overcame him, Satan, with the blood of the Lamb and by the word of their testimony, and they loved not their lives unto death."*

I don't recommend that we go around blurting out all sorts of dark secrets and difficult life situations to just anyone, anywhere. The damage that was done to us can be used for good—we can help many hurting people around us today. Our world is suffering. It is full of hurting people who need to know that they are not alone. They need to know how to get better, and have someone take them to the Healer where there is help for their suffering. God heals! He healed me and He can heal anyone who is willing to let Him.

Wright

How important is it for us to be emotionally healthy in our walk with God?

Trant

It's the place for true friendship and closeness with God. We've all had friends who would only let us get so close—he or she did not welcome a close friendship. Emotional healing allows us to let our walls down with God, giving Him access to those places that may have hurt us during our lives. We are able to sit with Him (bringing our past, present, and future) as we do our Bible study. We sit with Him in our pain and in our sorrow, and it creates a deep friendship and trust with God. Instead of shutting down, we "open up." As you said regarding forgiveness, is it okay "just to forget it?" No. I believe we should bring it with us as we sit with God. God can handle the things that upset and hurt us. They are a part of us and it is okay for us to hold them in our hands while He sits next to us. By being open with God, we deepen our friendship and trust with Him. This is how intimacy is developed in our friendship with God.

To be emotionally healthy in our walk with God will make us lead a more dynamic and happy life as believers of Jesus Christ.

Wright

Why should believers who feel they have no hurts bother going through a healing study or workshop?

Trant

There are a multitude of reasons. One would be to understand the suffering that others face. There are many people who don't have violent parents and weren't abused—none of the awful things that we hear on the news every day. If you consider yourself to be one of these individuals you are very valuable and needed. You will also benefit from emotional healing courses, even though you feel that you've never been hurt. You have great potential to reach out in ministry to those of us who have been wounded. You can equip yourself to help others, becoming able to understand a wide range of suffering that exists today. Obtaining wisdom and understanding, and learning how God heals will strengthen your ministry.

Another reason is to be enabled to accept the hurting people in our lives and to appreciate their strengths. We have the dilemma in our churches of, "What should I do? How can I help?" If believers will engage in studies that are meant to bring about emotional healing, they may also find a ministry and a place to serve God. They may come to enjoy an intense ministry and be privileged to watch the miracles that God does in peoples' lives. He really does rescue people from addictions, He really does rescue them from financial distress that maybe they created on their own and He rescues them from loneliness and depression. He even heals people who are physically ill, Jehovah Rapha is still here—He is a healer—a great physician and a wonderful counselor.

Is there no balm in Gilead? Is there no physician there? Why then is there no healing for the wound of my people? (Jeremiah 8:22.)

It is God who is asking these questions. He is frustrated with the lack of healing for His people because they refuse to go to the Physician and receive the cure. The obvious answer to each of God's questions is yes. Yes there is a balm in Gilead; yes there is a Physician there! God is asking why we are not going to Him, receiving the balm and being healed. He has given an answer for hurt and pain, for suffering of all kinds. We must believe and go to Jesus to get the cure.

It is hard to face suffering in our own lives. It is easier to stay protected and just keep it to ourselves. We may create a protective emotional boundary that no one can cross. We make sure we will never get hurt again, but we also make sure we will never get healed.

Whether you have faced abuse and suffering in your life or not, God can use you to help *others* to heal. It may be your own healing and it may be you helping someone else to heal. God will bless you by showing you how powerful He is. Study the Word of God, pray, get involved with other Christians in structured studies and prayer groups. He really is Jehovah Rapha—He really is the Great Healer. He wants you to join Him in the journey—your own or that of someone else.

Wright

Today we have been talking with DeBee Trant. She is a motivational Christian author and speaker, and, as we have found today through her own personal story and background, she is able to help others learn to be more grounded and to have more intimate relationships, not only with Jesus Christ, but with others as well.

DeBee, thank you so much for being with us today on *Remarkable Women of Faith!*

Trant

David, I would like to leave your readers with a little encouragement and hope. One of the interesting things that I incorporate into my ministry is S.O.A.P. You may have heard that acronym before, it is not a new one. To make it more effective in my own life and to encourage others, I also make my own old fashioned lye soap. I give it to supporters of the ministry and those who attend our events. It is made by me in various forms and is completely natural with no animal products. With my soap you learn the S.O.A.P. method of studying God's Word:

Spiritual Washing Instructions

S   Scripture   _____

O   Observation   _____

A   Application   _____

P   Prayer   _____

Read the Scripture you have chosen to focus on. Read it in context (not one or two verses). Write your Scripture reference next to the letter S.

Make an observation about the passage you read and come to a conclusion about it. Write your observation next to the letter O.

Make what you study apply to your life. This is very important. Write the application next to the letter A.

Pray about what you studied and ask God to help you to heal through the study of His Word and to give you wisdom as you continue to face tough issues in your life. Ask Him to show you what the next step is for you to continue to heal. It is very helpful for you to write out what you are praying for and the date you prayed.

If you were with me right now I would give you a bookmark with this acronym on it and some Scripture to work on. A good beginning is to study the word "heal" or "healing." You can use your Bible concordance and begin with some of the New Testament references.

I would also give you a bar of my personally handmade soap. I call it "Scripture soap," because it comes with a Scripture to focus on. This would be my encouragement to you. Soap can clean the outside but S.O.A.P. will clean the inside where God says it really counts.

To begin a healing journey you must:

1. Make the *sacrifice* of *time*.
2. *Accept* that you need *help*.
3. Get *involved* in the *study* of God's Word.
4. Be *willing* to *fellowship* with like-minded believers.
5. *Begin* to *pray* on a regular basis.

May the God of all comfort comfort all who are searching for answers and help them to begin the journey today—*stepping up*, one step at a time. Each step takes you closer to the great Physician, the wonderful Counselor, and the Balm in Gilead, our Redeemer and Healer. It has been a blessing to be with you. May God bless this Christian resource in the lives of all who read it.

Thank you to my friend, Charlotte, for her encouragement and help in completing this project.

About the Author

DeBee Trant is a wife, mother, and grandmother. She is also founder of Up Close Ministries, a non-profit 501(c)(3) charity. She is a contributing author of the *Refined by Fire* Christian series and is a sought-after motivational teacher and speaker. She is the Women's Director of Pine Valley Community Church in Pine Valley, California.

DeBee and her husband, Michael, have raised three of their own children and now are raising their three grandchildren. After the deaths of each of their mothers they also began taking full-time care of their brothers, Mark and Terry. DeBee's brother, Mark, is the twelfth of the twelve children born to her mom and dad. He was born with down syndrome and functions at about the eighteen-month-old level. Terry, Michael's brother, is fifty-four at the time of this writing and functions at about the eight-year-old level. Needless to say, they follow God's commands to provide for and nurture their family.

Up Close Ministries is dedicated to:
Spiritual Truths that Emotionally Heal
DeBee's life verse is:
"They overcame him by the blood of the lamb and by the word of their testimony." Revelation 12:11a (NIV).

Through her testimony and the Word of God, DeBee gives others hope and the chance for a new beginning. She is known for speaking on emotional and spiritual healing. Using visuals, she motivates others to journey into an intimate relationship with Jesus Christ.

DeBee Trant
Up Close Ministries
P.O. Box 338
Pine Valley, CA 91962
Phone: 619.889.7330
E-mail: debee@upcloseministries.org
www.upcloseministries.org

Chapter 13

KIM ZWEYGARDT

THE INTERVIEW

David Wright (Wright)
Today we are talking with Kim Zweygardt. "Passionate!" "Captivating!" Life-Changing!" all describe Kim Zweygardt's portrayals of women in Scripture. Kim is an author, dramatist, and the founder of Lamplight Ministries, which illuminates Scripture through drama. She has written five different first-person accounts of women whose lives were changed by meeting Jesus. She says, "It occurred to me that none of the women who encountered Christ wrote her own story. I have a faith story to tell so my question was, 'If I met this woman, what would she say about her encounter with Christ?' I try to answer that question through drama."

You've been included in the book as a remarkable woman of faith. Do you define yourself as a remarkable woman of faith?

Kim Zweygardt (Zweygardt)
The answer to that is both "yes" and "no." The Bible says that each one of us has been given a measure of faith. As a Christian I know that's true, but a lot of times I feel more like the story of Gideon

where he is hiding in the wine press threshing grain and the angel of the Lord appears to him and calls him a "mighty warrior of God" when he's in there hiding. That is the way this is. I know it's true because that's what the Bible says, but do I always feel like it and do I always live a remarkable life? I'm not so sure about that except for who I am in Christ. Only through Christ is my life remarkable!

Wright
Who does fall into that category in your life or who would you say you look up to as a woman of faith?

Zweygardt
The first person I think of is in my own family—my mom. My mom is one of those people who is a "glass is half full" person. She always has a very positive outlook. Even at times when life was very, very difficult, she maintained that very up-beat, positive outlook. I inherited some of that from her. Two examples are her relationship with my father and the way she was brought up. Her parents divorced at a time when people really didn't get divorced—when divorce was a scandalous thing—so she learned early to cope by keeping her faith.

I have a friend who is my mentor. Lonnie Frick is in her eighties. I always look at Lonnie and think, "That's who I want to be when I grow up!" She's one of those people who has this quiet, sweet spirit about her. She just loves God and she loves people. Through the trials of her eighty years she's been able to look to God to supply all of her needs; she's believing God even now. She believes God for the miracles needed in her family, in her children and then grandchildren and now even great grandchildren's lives. She has that "measure of faith" I mentioned earlier. You can see it in everything she does—in her countenance and in the way she interacts with people. I want to be like that!

Both Lonnie Frick and my mother are women I really look up to as remarkable women of faith.

Wright
You say you have a "faith story to tell." Will you tell me your story and how your ministry of dramatic portrayals of women from the Bible began?

Zweygardt

I'm the prodigal daughter. As I mentioned, my mom and dad's relationship was difficult, even though we were a very nice middle-class family. We went to church and Bible school so I got that foundation of faith. But things had happened to me as a child that affected me and how I reacted to the turmoil in my home and the difficulties between my mom and dad. All those things caused me to have a rebellious streak. I hit puberty during the '70s when sex, drugs, rock and roll, woman's rights, and all those things were prevalent. I started down this pathway of going my own way even though I had that foundational upbringing in the church. Through multiple marriages and abusive relationships I found myself farther and farther away from God.

The Bible says, "We all like sheep have gone astray," and I was a sheep! I heard an illustration one time that sheep are not really very smart. They just go wherever their appetites take them. When they're out in the pasture they begin to eat the grass. They just eat and eat, and as they're walking toward each new patch of grass they're working their way farther and farther from the shepherd until finally they look up and look around; they have wandered into an unsafe distance from the shepherd. That was me.

If you were to tell me then that I was going to do some of the things that I ended up doing I would have said, "Oh no; no way!" But gradually, through that step-by-step pathway away from God, I found myself in a position where I didn't know where to turn. In the world's eyes in most ways I appeared to have achieved success, but I was a girl with a broken heart. I had gone through multiple marriages, relationships that were physically abusive—emotionally and verbally abusive—and finally the Lord brought me to a place where I had no place else to turn.

I'm so grateful for that foundation of knowing Scripture—knowing that God was there—because when I was brought to the end of myself, I knew where to go back to. Really, I ended up throwing myself at the feet of God and saying, "I've done everything I know how to do to live life so that it doesn't hurt and I'm still making mistakes. I'm still failing and I don't know what else to do." And in His grace He reached down and loved me and saved me and brought me back to Him and began to restore me.

I've described it as having a gaping wound in my heart that I had tried to fill with everything—men, money, success, my job, shopping, and travel—all the things the world says will bring you comfort, will bring you success, will bring you a fulfilled life; but none of those things did it.

Instead, God began to heal me from the inside to the outside. He put Himself in that wound and began to heal up all the broken places of my life. That's why I can portray the women in Scripture who were so broken, rejected, and so hurt in their lives. In the same way that they met Him, I have met Him and I know that He is the restorer of broken hearts. I know that He is the only one who can satisfy in life. Because of that I'm able to bring all of those emotions and all that understanding into these portrayals of those hurting, broken women.

How did it all begin? I was standing in my kitchen listening to Christian radio and something was said initiating this idea that popped into my mind. I had a background in theater from high school and college and it really was my first love. I jotted down a few notes about the story of the woman at the well because that is so much my own story. I wrote what that drama might look like and what that woman might say. The fruition of my idea—my drama ministry—was like the Paul Harvey "the rest of the story."

The stories in Scripture are so brief. They were all written from the outside looking in. I'm so grateful that God inspired men to write the stories of these women as they wrote down the Holy Scriptures. I love the fact that God made sure that these women were included in the Bible. But it still is not the same as if that woman told the story herself. So that's the background—the basis.

That day I jotted a few notes and thought, "One of these days I'll write that down," but I never did. Then, several months later the Lord woke me up in the middle of the night. (I would like to be able to say that I always hear the voice of God when He speaks to me, but that's not true.) In this case there was no mistaking the voice of God. It was 3:33 in the morning when He woke me up and said, "Are you going to write it or not?" And I knew immediately what He was talking about. I hadn't even been thinking about it anymore. My life had gotten busy with other things but I knew immediately when He said those words that He was talking about this drama.

So at 3:33 in the morning I got up and sat down at the computer and the words just flowed. It was just divine inspiration from the Holy Spirit. I am a writer—you can give me a topic and I can come up with something that will be fairly decent to read, but this was different. There was no rewriting, no having to think about how to phrase the stories—it all came out all in one piece. In a couple of hours it was written and that was the beginning.

Wright

You define yourself as a "dramatist." How does that differ from being an actress?

Zweygardt

In some ways you could say it's the same. But I make that distinction just because actresses most often portray fictional characters, although sometimes they portray historical characters. "Dramatist" is a word that God gave me to define what I do so that it would be distinct from acting. It defines what I do in portraying a real woman who was a living, breathing person and who experienced this dramatic event that needs to be portrayed as opposed to someone acting out a fictional story. There might be some truth in that fictional story—some universal type of truth about love or death or whatever the subject might be—but the character has been invented by someone to tell that truth. In what I write about and portray, the character is real. The woman was real. I use the term "dramatist" to make a distinction that what I do is different to what you normally think of as acting.

Wright

What differences do you see between the women you portray and woman you meet every day?

Zweygardt

That's one of the great things about these dramas. It shows we're not all that different! I find that today's women respond to those women from long ago. Sometimes we look at Scripture and say, "Well gosh, that's a great story but that was so long ago that it really doesn't have anything to do with me." But I think seeing it dramatized brings us face to face with the fact that we really are still the same.

God created each one of us. We each one bear what has been termed the "fingerprint of God." We all bear the *Imago Dei*—we were made in the image of God. So really we're not so different. Our circumstances have changed; the cultural parts of our lives have changed and are different. We live in modern times versus Biblical times, but when you strip away what's on the outside, our needs are still the same. Our desires are the same. We all seek significance. We all seek love. We all seek to live a life that matters, that transcends the mundane and the everyday routines we deal with. So I think that the differences are cultural and time differences, but we are still in need of the same things because we were all created by the same God.

Wright

Is your ministry primarily directed at women or do you see men impacted by your portrayals?

Zweygardt

That has been a very interesting aspect of all of this. Obviously, as a woman who is portraying women, I thought of this as a woman's ministry. But I am often asked to do my portrayals to a mixed group, for example a church service. I'm always amazed at how very much men have been impacted by these dramas. Perhaps it's because men are very visual in their orientation. Perhaps seeing that portrayal makes them really see the pain of these women's circumstances for the first time. It's one thing to read about it and sometimes it becomes so familiar we just gloss over it.

For example, we say, "The woman at the well—here's this woman and she's had five husbands. What kind of woman is that?" And you move on without really seeing the whole story. I know from personal experience that you don't just get married five times for no reason. There's some kind of pain that drives that behavior—that act of looking for love in all the wrong places.

Because the portrayals are so visual, men can see the whole story. They "get" the pain that's there and they're not as willing to write it off like, "Yes, she was just a woman. That's just her story." They're brought more face-to-face with the emotions. Yes, my ministry is primarily to women, but men have been very deeply touched and impacted by these dramatic portrayals.

Wright

You are a very busy woman. You work full time as a Certified Registered Nurse Anesthetist (CRNA) and own your own corporation. You are involved in your church as a worship leader and in women's ministry. You are involved in your community in economic development and play the trumpet in a community band and sing in a community chorus. You have a husband and three children. You are writing a book, and you travel and perform these dramas. What drives you in all of these roles and how do you juggle all of it?

Zweygardt

I think it's the same thing that drives me in all places. My personal mission statement is to know Christ and make Him known through writing, music, and drama. That doesn't really answer the question about *all* of my different music interests or my interest in my community and economic development, my job and all those things, so let me explain it like this. Many people compartmentalize their life. This is their "job box" and this is their "family box" and here is their "faith box" and on and on. I see life as a grid system. As a Christian, my grid system is my faith. Instead of compartmentalizing my life, every part of my life fits into the faith grid. So wherever I go, whatever I'm doing, first and foremost it's not about me, it's about God.

My daughter just asked me a question about going on a mission trip versus going on a trip to Europe with a state singing group. She feels bad that she's not going as a missionary. I told her, "You know Lauren, you *are* going as a missionary because wherever we go we take Christ with us." So you can't really separate your faith from everything else. Whether I'm interacting with a patient in my role as a CRNA, whether I'm interacting with surgeons and the nursing staff, if I'm at church or if I'm playing my trumpet, if I'm not Christ-like in all those roles, then I have given the name of Christ a bad name. I don't want that.

My faith drives all the things I do—my faith is first and foremost. I'm just excited that God has given me all these different things to do. Sometimes it is a little hard to juggle everything. I have a tendency to over-commit myself to too many things, but its all just so much fun! That's how I justify it. That's how I'm able to do it all. It all really has to do with living out the life that Christ has given me to live and all the roles he has given me to live, to just bear His name and image in the world and to try to impact the people he puts in my path.

I find myself having spiritual conversations no matter where I am and I think that's because I am open to it. People know that I'm a Christian and so the subject of faith comes up and I can be a witness to others.

Wright

You've often quoted T. D. Jakes who says, "Your misery is your ministry." Could you explain that and how you relate to the women you portray?

Zweygardt

I love that quote because God doesn't waste anything. You look at your life sometimes and there are bad things that have happened or you want to ask "Why?" I look at my "colorful marital history" and wonder, "Why did all that happen?" Yet, because of that, I can speak to women who've made mistakes. I can speak to women who have been in abusive relationships.

It is just amazing how many times something will be said and I'll just know somehow that there's more to it than what is being said. With a few questions I'm able to guide that conversation and then the woman will say, "You know, I've never told anybody that."

I believe that God doesn't want to waste whatever pain you have experienced in your life. That pain is a refiner's fire to burn away what is not of Christ. We're all made in His image. We're all to become more and more Christlike in our lives. That's our purpose in life—to become more like Christ and to glorify God in our lives. So that means taking those things that have been the hardest things and then using them to empathize, to have love, and to have compassion for other people. In the same way, that is what is within the ministry with the women that I portray.

Christ comes to the woman at the well and offers her living water when she is hopeless. She's at that well all by herself. In those days, going to the well was a social event. But she is an outcast because of the culture in which she lives. Christ says. "I can offer you living water."

She cries out to Him, "Give me this water that I won't have to keep coming here to draw the water and might not thirst again."

Then He seems to change the subject and says, "Go and get your husband." I can just see her heart fall. It's like her hope has been pulled away from her suddenly. Everything is going to be taken care of and then He says to go and get her husband. She's thinking, "Well, here we go again. I'm not good enough. It's not for me."

And I know how that feels. I know how it feels to believe that the things of God are not for you because you've been too used up—you've been too damaged. But then you tell the truth to Christ when He comes to you and you realize it *is* for you, that no one is beyond the grace of God. So that most miserable part of my life—that most hurtful and embarrassing thing that I used to joke about to cover up the pain—God has turned into good for Him. He's turned it into a wonderful ministry where I have the opportunity to be the bearer of His living water to others. They can see that Jesus loves them and it doesn't matter where they've been. The water *is* for them; they just need to accept it and go on. Because I've been there, when they see me up on a stage, then they know there's hope for them.

Sometimes in the body of Christ we shoot our wounded. We're told if we've been hurt and damaged or sinned or we're the prodigal son or daughter. We're told that God will accept us but He doesn't really have a place for us to be prominent in ministry or to make a difference in the world. This ministry, demonstrates that yes, there is a place for you. It's as though God is saying, "I've done it for this woman, I've done it for Kim Zweygardt, and I'll do it for you."

Wright

What has been your greatest joy in ministry as well as your greatest struggle?

Zweygardt

To be transparent has been the most difficult struggle. There was a time in my life when if you wanted to know something about me, all you had to do was ask and I would "vomit" it all out—*all* the bad stuff. It was almost pathological; my intent was to tell you all this bad stuff and if you reject me that would be okay because I don't have a whole lot invested in my relationship with you. So just right off the bat, here's the stuff. Then the Lord showed me that I needed to be a little more careful about talking about my past because often people would make fun of it or judge me based on it and not give me a chance.

Now I've come full circle and the Lord is saying, "Okay, now you've got to talk about it again." It's no longer pathological; I'm talking about it as a ministry. I'm talking about it as a way of helping other women versus it being almost a challenge—I'm going to lay it all out here and you can reject me or not. Now it's a much softer thing. There still may be those who reject me and my story, but that's all right. I'm talking about these things because God is saying now's the time.

So that has been my greatest joy—to be able to be used by Him. It has also been my greatest struggle because of the fear of rejection or being judged. I've got three kids, a wonderful Godly husband and I think about them having to hear about my past. Transparency is at the same time a joy and a struggle.

Wright

What would you say are the components of a life of faith?

Zweygardt

A life of faith first and foremost has to be relationship driven. We have to realize that our life is not about us—our relationship to the world is as Christ bearers. Sometimes we want to stay in our little churches or stay in our little friendships with other people who believe as we do. We're not concerned enough about taking Christ out into the world. But we've got the best news in the world—God sent His Son to save us and that salvation is for everyone who believes. Yet we don't act that way sometimes. It seems like we have more messages about what not to do rather than being loving and joy filled.

First of all we must have a relationship with God. The Bible records the conversation a lawyer had with Jesus. He asked Jesus, "What's the greatest commandment?" Jesus said that the first and great commandment is to love God with your whole heart, soul, and mind and the second is to love others as you love yourself (Matthew 22:35–39). Those are still the greatest commandments for a life of faith—to live your life loving God and loving others and bearing His image out into the world where they can see Christ in you.

Wright

What do you want your legacy to be?

Zweygardt

To have lived well and to hear those words whenever my life ends, "Well done good and faithful servant," and to know that God has gifted me and that I'm not like the servant who went and buried his gift. I want to know that to the best of my ability, I believed God and lived a life of faith and lived well with great joy in all parts of my life—as a wife, a mother, a friend, a dramatist, writer, and trumpet player! When it's all said and done I want people to say, "Kim did all the things that God called her to do."

I love the verse found in Romans 8:28, ." . . all things work together for good to them that love God, to them who are the called according to His purpose." I love that verse on several different levels: One, that we all are called according to His purpose and two, all things work together for good. Not just some things, not the things I think are working together for good, even those things that seem like the worst things. If I will give those things to Him, He will work them for His glory and for my good.

Another verse that is very, very meaningful to me is Ephesians 1:4. Here is my paraphrase of it: before God laid the foundation of the world He knew me—He knew Kim Zweygardt and He wrote my name in the Book of Life. That is such a precious verse to me because knowing that I would mess up, knowing that I would fall short, knowing that so often for so long in my life I would make the wrong choices, He still chose me and knew me before I knew Him and He wrote my name in the Book of Life. I love that. It colors everything in my life that He would choose me and He chose me knowing that I would make wrong choices. It just blows my mind and that's where my faith comes from. If He could do that for me, then whatever I do for Him is small in comparison.

Wright

What a great conversation. I really appreciate all the time you've spent with me today to answer all these questions. It's been enlightening and I really appreciate it.

Zweygardt

Thank you, David.

About the Author

KIM ZWEYGARDT is a dramatist, writer, and musician. Founder of Lamplight Ministries, Kim has captivated audiences across the United States as she illuminates the Holy Scriptures through drama. Kim's books include: *Stories from the Well*, *Chicken Soup for the Soul* (the *Healthy Living Series on Heart Disease* section), and she is a contributing author to *The Rocking Chair Reader* anthology, *Family Gatherings*. Her blog is available at www.kimzweygardt.com where she writes about faith, love, and life in the fast lane. Kim is a Certified Registered Nurse Anesthetist (CRNA) and the owner of Moonlight Anesthesia, PA. She graduated with honors from Samford University, Birmingham, Alabama. She is a member of the International Speakers Network and featured on www.bookaspeaker.net, www.ministrywomen.net, and www.womenspeakers.com.

Kim Zweygardt
Lamplight Ministry
P.O. Box 921
Saint Francis, KS 67756
Phone: 785.332.2487
E-mail: kim@kimzweygardt.com
www.kimzweygardtcom

Chapter 14

JENNIFER CURTET

THE INTERVIEW

David Wright (Wright)
Today we are talking with Jennifer Curtet. Jennifer Curtet is burning up the highways across the country with her high-energy keynotes and workshops. She is an authority in the areas of communication, customer service, leadership, motivation and attitude. Jennifer's contagious personality and cutting edge information has changed the way people communicate and live their lives. She delivers seminars packed with real-world, practical skills, tempered with her own engaging mixture of warmth and humor. As a speaker and author, Jennifer is a master storyteller and is sure to leave you breathless and inspired.

As Christians we are granted the blessed promise of everlasting life. What is the most coveted and significant promise you have ever received?

Jennifer Curtet (Curtet)
Wouldn't you know it—I finally got my dad (Dave) to promise to go with me to check out my new church and that was the very day he

was admitted into the hospital. "Likely excuse," I joked with him as he lay in his sterile hospital bed; but privately I was worried to my very core. Officially, that was the only promise he made to me, in thirty-three years, that was ever broken.

The first promise that had the most impact on me came when I was three. At a very young age, unfortunately, I had been exposed to loss through the divorce of my biological parents. Seemingly to everyone, however, I was fine—I was young enough to not be overly affected by our new situation and naturally magnanimous enough to be accepting of all the new partners and family members who entered our lives.

When Dave came into the picture to date my mom he was an instant hit. He was a fun-loving and free-spirited hippy with the greatest wild, curly black hair we had ever seen! He adored our Mom and it seemed as if the balance was being restored in our little family. Most importantly though, Dave was willing to roughhouse with us and make my brother Bill and me the center of his world at a moments notice. From his racy, orange Chevy Camaro to his beautiful, sage green eyes—we loved him immediately.

Secretly, I was determined to have him fall as deeply for me as I had for him. I did everything I could to win Dave over: I sang my heart out in private concerts for him on the fireplace hearth, I wore special party dresses even though I hated anything "girlie" and I—the pickiest eater on the planet—ate strange, spicy foods; all of this to win over his affection!

A few months into my new conquest, I insisted that Dave be the one to say my bedtime prayers with me. During this special time the two of us went through each one, hand-in-hand, reciting them together. I realize now that this must have absolutely melted his heart.

When the prayers were over and it was time to say goodnight and turn out the light I grabbed Dave and asked him with desperate eyes and a humble spirit, "Are you going to leave me like my daddy did?" Just a few short months into all of our lives, Dave looked me squarely in the eye and promised he would never leave.

> Jesus said, "Whoever humbles himself like this child is
> the greatest in the kingdom of Heaven"—*Matthew 18:4.*

As Christians we have received the same promise from God. As we walk in the Truth and live honorably as Christ did, we will be the receivers of the holist gift of all: we will be forgiven of our sins and given everlasting life. Through Him and with Him we are able to live forever, knowing we will never be orphaned. Ultimately we, the children of the Lord, are given "the promise" that He will never leave us.

The magnitude of this holy Gift is terribly and unfortunately minimized. As one of His children and a believer in Jesus Christ as the Son of God, I am forgiven of all sins and forever protected and loved. I am able to breathe in the glory of deep, resonating peace and stability knowing that I will never be forsaken, never be forgotten, and never be left behind.

As a little girl, on some level, I felt "left behind" and unimportant when I was left by my biological father. As my brother and I would wait for him to arrive for our weekends and fulfill grandiose promises, we were consistently disappointed and made to believe that there were other things that were more important than we were. But when I knew that I was wanted and cherished by Dave it was the greatest message to my starving and forsaken heart—I was worthy of his love.

Just as Dave promised to love me and stand by me, God has made the same promise to his children on earth—we are worthy of His love! We must celebrate, knowing how loved and cherished we are and live completely self-assured of our immeasurable value within the sacred place of His heart. Our loving Father promises to protect us and raise us up in glory and to bestow upon us the richness of His love, His truth, and His forgiveness.

"If you love me, you will obey what I command. And I will ask the Father, and he will give you another Counselor to be with you forever—the Spirit of truth. The world cannot accept him, because it neither sees him nor knows him. But you know him, for he lives with you and will be in you. I will not leave you as orphans; I will come to you. Before long, the world will not see me anymore, but you will see me. Because I live, you also will live. On that day you will realize that I am in my Father, and you are in me, and I am in you. Whoever has my commands and obeys them, he is the one who loves me. He who loves me will be loved by my Father, and I too will love him and show myself to him"—*John 14:18.*

Wright

As Christians, the highest compliment to our Heavenly Father is to live like Christ did. How do we live and testify daily that we are God's children?

Curtet

Dave was our father, our counselor, our hero, and our guide. Throughout our lives, for every major event, he was enthusiastically and proudly cheering us on from the sidelines.

It was time for the annual Father-Daughter Dance, which of course was a big, big deal to me. The dance that year had a 1920s flapper theme and I remember that my mom had painstakingly, and somewhat begrudgingly, sewn a beautiful orange flapper style dress for me to wear. At the time, money was tight in our home, which led to Dave working late nights on a regular basis to help make ends meet for our little family. This habit of getting home late had me worried sick that night, but he promised that he would make it home in time for our "date."

To my absolute surprise and delight, Dave showed up—as promised—decked out from head-to-toe in a rented "zoot suit" costume, complete with fedora, shined shoes, and a cane! The two of us spent that entire night—our date—dancing to every song. I was flipped and twirled, thrown through his legs and then tossed high into the air while all of the other little girls looked on longingly at my wonderful dad! Life was forever full of surprises like these from our "Davey-Baby." He was always everyone's favorite guy and somehow he always made everybody feel like they were the most trusted and valuable person in his life. Dave was the rarest of souls who accepted everyone, without reservation. He lightened the darkest of moods and softened the hardest of hearts. He was a blessing.

> "Blessed are those you choose and bring near to live in your courts!
> We are filled with the good things of your house,
> of your holy temple"—*Psalm 65:4.*

Sometimes I think my dad was in a hurry to pass on his knowledge, to share his heart. He was always reaching out, trying to fix everything, determined to teach.

Does the soul intuitively know that it doesn't have much time? I think of the short life of Christ and I'm humbled by the urgency and passion in which his message was shared. When we think of Jesus the man, with His gentle heart and genuine love for others, we learn of a selfless man who attracted and enchanted the masses. He loved the loveless, healed the sick, and inspired the broken spirits—He was a man of the people in the truest sense. He lived without reservation, without fear, without resentment. Because of His trust and unyielding love for His Father and His promise to free His children, He paid the ultimate price. For a man with so much to give, He lived rejected and alone in order to fulfill His promise to us. As His children, I believe it is our duty to pass on the Spirit in which He lived, as well as the Word that He spoke.

"The Spirit himself testifies with our spirit
That we are God's children"—*Romans 8:16.*

It is our responsibility to pass on the wisdom and grace that has been bestowed upon us. It is our calling to leave this world better than when we entered into it. We have been graced with an immeasurable gift and I believe the highest form of compliment to our Father comes through worship, dedication, and a servant's heart that is willing to teach those who are a step behind. What a beautiful tribute to strive to live like Jesus, every day, with every encounter.

"Be imitators of God, therefore, as dearly loved children and live a life of love, just as Christ loved us and gave himself up for us as a fragrant offering and sacrifice to God"—*Ephesians 5:1–2.*

Wright
What has been the most meaningful story you have learned within your Bible studies over the years?

Curtet
Leading up to my dad's hospitalization, I had been studying the Prodigal Son. It became very clear to me that the biblical story very closely, and almost eerily, modeled my dad's life. He thought he could figure it all out on his own using logic. Dave always needed proof, searching for truth in history and statistics until he finally realized that what had been missing from his life for some time was faith. He had been raised a Christian, but had fallen away from the church and had most recently started expressing a need to renew his faith and his spirit. Again, I can't help wonder now what the soul knows . . .

God says,

"In the time of my favor I heard you,
and in the day of salvation I helped you.
I tell you, now is the time of God's favor,
now is the day of salvation"—*2 Corinthians 6:2.*

While in the hospital, Dave's prognosis was grim. What was thought to be a little blockage turned out to be an eight-and-a-half-inch growth on his kidney that more than doubled in thirty-six hours.

However bad the news, he was optimistic and hopeful that he could beat this. At a low moment when it was just the two of us, Dave asked me to return a life's worth of promises in a favor to him: he wanted me to promise that I would be his confidant throughout his ordeal and allow him to vent his fear and anger. He also asked that I stand by any decision he made and ensure that his wishes were carried out, regardless of what the family thought would be in his best interest. My heart broke as I read between the lines of his request. Of course, I promised. How could we go on without Dave? How could he give up hope so easily? How would I find the strength to hold steadfast to what I had just promised him?

Strengthen the feeble hands, steady the knees that give way;
Say to those with fearful hearts, 'Be strong, do not fear;
Your God will come' "—*Isaiah 35:3–4.*

I know that we are only given what we can handle and that we are only brought *to* what we can get *through.* But that day, full of remorse and sadness, I fully understood the sheer magnitude of upholding your promise when you've given your word. Oh, what a test of honor and will to be burdened with such information, without breaking your oath!

When I think of the lifetime of promises that my dad upheld, it's such a testament to the character of the man. When I think of the agony and humiliation that the Lord endured for my salvation, all to uphold his promise, it's almost too much to bear. A promise is a binding oath and when it's forsaken it destroys the integrity of the foundation. I knew that day that I would stand by my father's wishes and support his decisions in his last moments of life. I placed my father's life and my faith in God's hands and knew that I would be carried though this trial in His grace.

"Do not fear, for I am with you;
do not be dismayed, for I am your God.
I will strengthen you and help you;
I will uphold you with my righteous right hand"—*Isaiah 41:10*.

Wright

Is it ever too late to confess your love of Christ? If we believe in our heart that Jesus Christ is the Son of God and died for our sins will we be forgiven in our final hours?

Curtet

Later that afternoon, my sister-in-law, Emi, was having a heart-to-heart with Dave. Since joining our family, the two of them had always been "thick as thieves" and Dave thought of Emi as one of his own. It was a rare and beautiful relationship that had been cultivated during intimate moments such as this one. There were never any boundaries with the two of them and no subject was ever off limits. During their conversation Emi boldly and unabashedly asked Dave, as he lay in the hospital, if he had accepted Christ into his heart, to which he immediately confirmed he had. Emi prodded saying, "Are you sure Dave?" and he answered, "I promise."

"That if you confess with your mouth, 'Jesus is Lord,' and believe in your heart that God raised him from the dead, you will be saved. For it is with your heart that you believe and are justified, and it is with your mouth that you confess and are saved"—*Romans 10:9–10*.

Looking back on these snapshots of moments that still, one year later seem frozen in time, I can see the progression of the Lord's work. There is no coincidence or happenstance in the stirring of my dad's heart, or the hunger in his soul to reacquaint himself with his faith. The sense of peace that Emi bestowed upon our family with the telling of Dave's salvation was like a beacon of light for us in the midst of our greatest darkness as a family.

We were constantly given gifts of grace throughout this period of mourning that helped us feel comfort and peace during the worst season of our lives. Through God's promise to guard our hearts and minds and take our pain from us to create comfort, we've been blessed with a sense of protection and eternal encouragement that has carried us.

Jesus said, "Blessed are the peacemakers,
For they will be called sons of God"—*Matthew 5:9.*

Wright

Does the soul intuitively know when the end is near?

Curtet

Our darkest moments were yet to come. Six days into the battle we were told that my dad was septic and needing dialysis. It was confirmed that he had renal cell cancer and it was too far gone to do much of anything for him. Our options were grim—we could either do nothing and let the cancer run it's course and put Dave through possible trauma in this last moments of life or we could put up a temporary fight and start the dialysis.

To start the dialysis they would have to intubate him in order for his heart to withstand the treatment. Seems like an easy enough choice, except that the doctor told us there was only a 10 percent chance that he would ever be strong enough to breathe again after he was intubated. We were tormented at these options—truthfully, they didn't seem like options at all.

To add to this pressure, I had the added weight of a promise to uphold to my dad—I told him I wouldn't let anyone perform any heroics. I ran to my dad's room and told him through tears, with very little detail, what had to be done to get his dialysis going. Without any fear he responded, "Let's do it. I want all my options."

"You came near when I called you,
And you said, 'Do not fear.'
O Lord, you took up my case;
You redeemed my life"—*Lamentations 3:57–58.*

We gave the doctors the green light to start the dialysis. We knew that this meant we would never be able to talk to our "Davey-Baby" again. To say it was it was our darkest hour doesn't come close to describing the sheer agony of what we had to allow the doctors to do. We were given our time to say goodbye, although we never told Dave that he may not come back from the intubation. We felt that we were sparing him the fear and agony that we as a family decided to carry for him. Since then, we've struggled with this, wondering if we should have told him of his impending doom. Should we have been brutally honest and told him that one way or another he was going to die soon?

> "Brothers, since we have confidence to enter
> The Most Holy Place by the blood of Jesus . . .
> Let us draw near to God with a sincere heart
> in full assurance of faith, having our hearts
> sprinkled to cleanse us from a guilty conscience
> and having our bodies washed with pure water"—*Hebrews 10:19, 22.*

And then I go back to the question: does the soul know that it doesn't have much time? As we stood in the room sobbing and loving Dave with everything we had left in us, there was a strange peace and calm within him. He and my mom, who were still a beautiful, loving couple after thirty-three years, had some sweet moments together. Then Dave wanted to kiss everyone goodbye.

When I couldn't contain my heartache and tears he asked me, "What's wrong baby?" and all I could say was, "I just want you to go home!" Of course, we assumed that he was only aware that we were saying goodbye for the night, but I believe he knew—in his soul—that he was saying goodbye for good. With a grin on his face, my dad said, "I *am* going home, I promise."

> "God will wipe every tear from their eyes.
> There will be no more death or mourning or
> crying or pain, for the old order of things
> has passed away"—*Revelation 21:4.*

Wright
Do miracles exist, even in the darkest moments of our despair?

Curtet
After the dialysis had failed and our worst fears had become a reality, we realized that we needed to take my dad off the respirator—no heroics. As a family we gathered around Dave as he struggled for almost an hour to breathe without the aid of machines, to no avail. Our eyes were focused on the heart monitor that held the last glimmer of hope that we may have a miracle to celebrate if he regained consciousness. There were eight of us in the room and as the monitor's statistics started to drop rapidly our hearts plummeted. There would be no miracle today. We prayed over him, cried over him, mas-

saged his shoulders, and just loved him with everything we had left. As we all had our hands placed on his body wishing him Godspeed, his eyes opened! His eyes were the color of electric green—the most beautiful bright emerald I have ever seen! They were literally neon as he looked up to the heavens. My brother, his wife, Emi, and I witnessed the entire event, and to our surprise no one else saw it.

> The Lord replied, 'My Presence will go
> with you and I will give you rest' "—*Exodus 33:14.*

I am convinced that we got our miracle that day. I know that we were in the presence of the Lord and that we were witness to Dave's final promise of going Home. We were given one final gift. From the moment Dave entered into our lives he was the light in our darkness, truly the greatest gift in all of our lives. And even though it sometimes feels like we'll never find that light again, we are steadfast in our faith and know that we will be reunited again in the Kingdom of Heaven. Like it says in Hebrews, faith is being sure of what we hope for and certain of what we do not see. Through God's promise and mercy we will be together again, I am certain.

Wright
How do we endure when the load seems too heavy to bear?

Curtet
I do my best every day to live as Jesus did. I reach out to others with a servant's heart, I love the unlovable without judgment or contempt, and I persevere with grace, even in my darkest hours. As a child of God's promises I work to clothe myself in compassion, kindness, humility, gentleness, and patience. I remind myself of the promises that I make in my faith to God the Father every day because after all, that's what keeps one foot moving in front of the other. As I work to restore peace in others' hearts I find that God is, in that process healing mine. So as I slowly heal I hold steadfast to one last promise:

> "Let the beloved of the Lord rest secure in Him,
> for He shields him all day long,
> and the one the Lord loves rests
> between His shoulders"—*Deuteronomy 22:12.*

Emerald Eyes

A life of mine I will not erase,
The race begins yet I'm tired of the chase.
A time ago that can't be forgotten,
His tender fruit has grown stale and rotten,
My father's gone and left me adrift,
From this loss the Lord prepares my gift.
He promised to rescue me from my demise,
His creed was etched in his emerald eyes.
His gentle hand lifted me from the ground,
Brushed me off and straightened my frown.
Softly whispering he began to teach,
Of things I believed were out of reach;
Filled me up with all I'd bear,
But most of all he was always there.
But the sands of time fell from his glass,
As he had wished we let him pass.
A promise kept as he went,
Without a doubt he was heaven sent.
Out of darkness my spirits lift,
Self-assured while the Lord prepares my gift.
Head upright I gaze to the skies,
In loving memory of emerald eyes.

—William Sterling Buck II

About the Author

JENNIFER CURTET is the president of Aristocrat Enterprises, Inc., a personal and professional training firm in Las Vegas, Nevada. Her business, which was started with her husband Ludovic who is a personal trainer, is committed to the development of the heart, mind, body, and soul of today's leader. Jennifer has coached countless individuals on issues such as superior leadership and management skills, exceptional customer service, life balance and stress reduction, effective communication skills, and cultivating winning attitudes. She has written three books: *The Princess Principle, Ordinary Women... Extraordinary Success, and The Art of Being Assertive*, which is now available on audio CD.

Over the last ten years as a professional speaker, Jennifer has conducted consulting assignments, training workshops, and keynote speeches for such renowned organizations as: Coca-Cola, Wal-Mart, Johnson & Johnson, Boeing, Rockwell Collins, Honeywell, Blue Cross Blue Shield, Johns Hopkins University, Price Waterhouse Coopers, Cisco Systems, Western Union, Heinz, Verizon Wireless, Washington Mutual, and the U.S. Department of Defense, just to name a few. Regardless of the industry or company Jennifer is working with, she is committed to branding her quality leadership at every level of the organization.

Jennifer's passion and persistence have activated the hearts and minds of hundreds of thousands to rise up and fulfill their destiny. Her strength and conviction on the platform have earned her standing ovations and rave reviews around the world. Her spunk and energy have made her a crowd favorite at conferences and events that draw tens of thousands of people. As a wife, daughter, sister, and friend, Jennifer is an inspiration to those who know her and a wonderful example of Servant Leadership in action. As a Christian, she is committed to living the "Jesus Style" as she reaches out to others in order to make a positive impact on their lives and to be a powerful force in this world.

Jennifer Curtet
Aristocrat Enterprises, Inc.
Phone: 602.421.8653
www.Jennifercurtet.com
www.aristocratenterprises.com